Past-into-Present Series

PRISONS

Rosamund Morris

B.T.BATSFORD LTD
London

First published 1976
© Rosamund Morris, 1976

ISBN 0 7134 3242 X

Printed in Great Britain by
The Anchor Press, Tiptree, Essex
for the Publishers, B. T. Batsford Ltd,
4 Fitzhardinge Street, London W1H 0AH

Acknowledgment

The Authors and Publishers would like to thank the following for their kind permission to reproduce copyright illustrations: the British Library for fig 5; the Central Office of Information, London, for fig 57; the Greater London Council Print Collection for fig 33; the Keystone Press Agency for figs 49, 51, 52, 53, 54, 55, 56, 58; the London Museum for fig 50; the Mansell Collection for figs 10, 23, 24, 25, 26, 28, 35, 36, 46; the Parker Gallery, London, for fig 8; the Pierpont Morgan Library for fig 1; the Press Association Limited for fig 59; and the Victoria and Albert Museum for figs 22, 45. The other pictures appearing in this book are the property of the Publishers.

Contents

The Illustrations

Introduction

'Prison' for most people means Holloway, Wormwood Scrubs or the local gaol. But it should not be thought of solely in these terms. A prison is simply a place in which people are held captive. An aeroplane when hijacked becomes a prison for those held hostage in it. The journalist or political leader held under house arrest in a foreign country suddenly becomes a prisoner in the familiar surroundings of his own home.

Prisons have existed for a very long time. About 3,000 years before Christ, the idea of prison was expressed in the cuneiform or wedge-shaped writing of the Sumerians by a combination of the symbols for 'dark' and 'house'. Archaeologists are still finding new evidence about imprisonment in the ancient world.

From earliest times, imprisonment has served a variety of purposes. It has been used by kings and governments and private individuals to stifle political opposition, to suppress those who constitute a threat to society, to provide cheap labour, or simply for personal gain. Wars, too, have throughout history produced their own forms of imprisonment with the taking of hostages, the capture of fighting men, and the subjection of people living in occupied countries. It is, however, in the legal process of arrest, trial and punishment for law-breakers that imprisonment has come to play an increasingly significant role throughout the world.

This book outlines the main features of British prison history from medieval times to the present day. Running through what is broadly speaking a chronological account are three main strands. First of all, the book seeks to show how a motley collection of prisons has gradually been extended and developed into the national prison system we have today. Secondly, it is concerned with the often appalling conditions in which prisoners were kept and with the efforts of prison reformers to improve them. Finally, it reflects something of the changing attitudes towards the treatment of offenders and the continuing debate about the aims and value of imprisonment.

1
Prisons in the Middle Ages

The First Prisons

Imprisonment was used in England a long time before the first written evidence of it appears in the ninth century. The early prisons were nothing like the great, walled buildings with which we are familiar today. An Anglo-Saxon prison was probably little more than a rough shed, or a room in the great house of king or noble, which could be securely fastened and guarded. King Alfred the Great (871-899) has left us this description which shows how a prison room might have formed part of the great house. In 'all kings' residences: some men are in his chamber, some in the hall, some on the threshing-floor, some in prison'.

The prisoners included personal enemies of the king or noble, hostages and prisoners of war. Very rarely indeed were they ordinary law-breakers. Other methods were used to deal with people who committed crimes. All serious criminals (including thieves) were put to death. Lesser offenders were fined and ordered to pay compensation to the victim. They might also be mutilated, branded or whipped. For instance, a convicted forger usually had a hand cut off and nailed above the door of the mint as a gruesome warning to others. Occasionally, people awaiting trial by ordeal were 'imprisoned' in the stocks and this practice became more common in the first half of the eleventh century. But generally speaking, imprisonment had very little part to play in a still primitive society which preferred to think of punishment in terms of 'an eye for an eye, a tooth for a tooth'.

This harsh and unyielding attitude towards crime was to change little over the centuries. Throughout the Middle Ages, death, mutilation, various forms of corporal punishment and fines were the standard penalties.

After the Norman Conquest of 1066, the Normans tried to strengthen their position in England by building massive castles, and indirectly provided for the first time buildings suitable for use as prisons. Both kings and barons made use of their castle dungeons to imprison their personal enemies — but with no legal right to do so. At the same time, there was a growing tendency to use imprisonment, legitimately, for holding accused persons in custody to await trial.

1 A mass execution in the Middle Ages. Bodies suspended from the gallows were a grim reminder of the fate which awaited criminals.

Medieval Prisons

The first signs of this development can be seen in the eleventh century. At this time, the sheriffs (the king's officers in the counties) were made responsible for the safekeeping until trial of all suspected offenders. The sheriffs were not obliged to set up their own gaols, but many did so.

In 1166, an attempt was made to organize these sheriffs' prisons on a firmer basis. At the Assize of Clarendon, it was decreed that gaols were to be built 'in every county where none existed' and that the sheriffs were to 'ensure the close

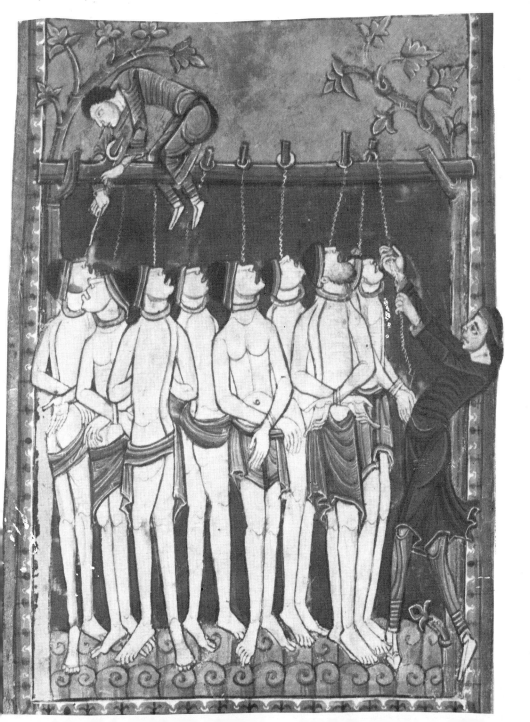

keeping of prisoners in these gaols'. By the time Henry III came to the throne in 1216, there were gaols in nearly all the counties. The sheriffs' prisons were the foundation of our prison system, and became known as *county gaols*. However, they were not the only kind of prison.

In the Middle Ages, kings often granted private individuals the right to have a prison. These became known as *franchise prisons*. An important landowner might have several such prisons. Ownership of a prison was a medieval status symbol, and the privilege was eagerly sought.

Town or borough corporations also had the right to have prisons and by the end of the sixteenth century virtually no town was without a gaol. In the Middle Ages the church was an important institution, and its officers, archbishops, bishops and other high-ranking churchmen, also maintained their own gaols. Members of the clergy had the right to be tried by a Church Court. This was known as 'Benefit of Clergy'. Any prisoner who claimed Benefit of Clergy had to prove his identity. Since few people apart from churchmen could read, a reading test (usually the first verse of the 51st Psalm) became the accepted means of determining whether or not the prisoner was entitled to Benefit of Clergy. If he passed the test, the prisoner was then handed over to the church authorities for trial. This could make the difference between life and death, since the Church Courts never imposed the death penalty.

Prisons in London

Several of the London prisons became in time 'national' prisons. This development was hastened when the king's courts became firmly established in London and when more and more litigants sought to bring their case before the royal justices.

The Tower of London Foremost among the royal palaces, the Tower is believed to have been the first building in London to have been used as a prison. Later, it became a state prison for political offenders. In the Middle Ages, it was also used as a prison for criminals and for prisoners in whom the king had a special interest, such as, for example, the Jews, who were under the special protection of the king until their expulsion in 1290.

The Fleet Until Newgate was built, the Fleet (so called because of its position on the banks of the Fleet stream) was known as 'the Gaol of London'. The date of its founding is not known, but it was probably in existence by 1130. It was the first purpose-built gaol in London. Most of its prisoners were debtors.

Newgate Destined to become the most notorious prison in London — and indeed in the whole of England — was Newgate, later called the 'English Bastille'. Newgate was built in 1188 by two carpenters and a blacksmith, at a cost of under £4. It speedily became the prison to which the most serious criminals were sent.

Two other prisons, established in Southwark in the 1370s, deserve a mention. They were the *King's Bench Prison* and the *Marshalsea*. Both of them later became famous as prisons for debtors. Prisoners either awaiting trial or who had been tried at the king's central courts were held there.

Prison Architecture

Unfortunately, few contemporary illustrations have survived to show us what medieval gaols looked like. We do know, however, that they were generally built of wood. For instance, records show that the gaols at Aylesbury, Oxford and Wallingford were built with wood taken from the nearby forests. Later on in the Middle Ages, stone, bricks and mortar were used. Prison roofs were tiled, slated or even thatched.

Not all medieval gaols were castle dungeons. Even so-called 'castle gaols' were often no more than makeshift shacks built within and against the castle's outer wall; they could easily be dismantled if the castle were needed for defence. Town gaols were usually quite tiny. Sometimes a single room in a local inn was commandeered for the purpose. In Norwich, the cellars below the Guildhall served as a prison when necessary. Larger prisons, and those which formed part of a castle keep or town gatehouse usually comprised several rooms. Such prisons would have had a basement with one or more floors above.

The basement section of a prison was called the dungeon and was generally reserved for the worst type of criminal. Dungeons were often just pits specially excavated for the purpose. They were usually sealed off at the top by a trap-door (as at Pevensey Castle), with a flight of steps or a ladder below. Above the pit was a gaol 'chamber'. Larger prisons had many of these chambers.

2 Castles were frequently used to house prisoners. This early medieval picture shows captives being released from their cells.

3 Men in prison and in the stocks (c. 1130-1174). Many medieval gaols were simple structures, built against town or castle walls. The stocks were used for minor offenders and public nuisances.

Prison Equipment

Medieval prison records contain references to the purchase of various items of equipment. Foremost among these were the stocks. 'Pairs' of stocks were often built to accommodate more than one person, but Stafford gaol must have achieved something of a record with one set of stocks almost 10 metres long! Stocks were usually installed inside the prison cells. However, the fact that, in December 1383, the gaoler of Salisbury Castle was accused of allowing prisoners in the stocks to die from exposure suggests that in some cases the prison stocks were placed outside.

Every gaol spent a certain amount on 'irons'. Collars and chains were used for securing prisoners round the neck. Fetters were for the legs and manacles for the hands. Chains to secure both ankles and wrists were called shackles. Regular purchases of all these were recorded — 33 pairs of fetters for Guildford in 1295, 12 for Huntingdon in 1365-6, 4 for Hertford in 1509-11 and so on. Prisoners were frequently kept in irons and even led to court in them in order to prevent them from escaping. It is difficult to believe that the iron shoes and thumb irons known to have been at Hertford in 1509-11 were for any other purpose than torture.

Medieval Gaolers

The most important official in any prison was the gaoler. Although the owner or controller of the gaol was in theory responsible for the management of the prison, in practice he had little or nothing to do with its day-to-day running. This duty fell to the gaoler or keeper, who either bought the appointment or was given it by the owner in return for a percentage of the proceeds. Gaolers were paid miserable wages — and often none at all. Despite this, there was never a shortage of applicants. In some families, gaol-keeping became hereditary.

Most gaolers ran their prisons as business concerns and tried to make as much profit out of their prisoners as they could. It gradually became customary to demand a fee from prisoners either when they were admitted to the gaol or when they were released. In some gaols, fees were demanded on both occasions. Such extortions did not always go unnoticed. Edmund le Lorimer, keeper of Newgate, was dismissed in 1319 partly because he had demanded excessive fees.

Prison Conditions

Prisoners were expected to provide all their own necessities — food, drink, bedding, clothing, even candles and fuel for a fire. If a prisoner had to languish in prison a long time before trial he might become bankrupt in the process. The possessions of one Yorkshireman, for example, were valued at nothing because he was said to have 'eaten them' while in prison. One can readily imagine how an unscrupulous gaoler could profit from a situation in which every prisoner was at his mercy. In many gaols, gaolers set up shop. They brewed beer and baked bread which the prisoners could buy — at a price. The authorities tried to stop this kind of profiteering. City of London aldermen in 1370 forbade the brewing of beer and the retailing of food in Newgate. By 1393, it seems they had accepted the inevitable. The regulations were then altered so that the keeper could sell food and drink, with the weak proviso that he should not charge exorbitant prices. From time to time, attempts were

4 A prisoner being made ready for interrogation. Already manacled, he is now being fettered by his gaoler.

5 This picture, from a fifteenth century French manuscript, depicts the release of two important political prisoners. Note the bunch of keys — an international symbol of the gaol-keeper's power.

6 The town gaol was part of everyday life. Passers-by could talk to the prisoners and give them alms.

made to regulate fees. In London, a maximum fee for the removal of irons was set at £5, a fairly large sum by contemporary standards. But there was no means of enforcing the regulations, and abuses continued.

In the larger prisons, it became customary to segregate paupers from those who could afford to pay for their comforts. Apart from this, prisoners were normally segregated according to the seriousness of their offence, and often protested when they were not. In 1314, a prisoner at Newgate complained that he had been wrongly placed in the depths of the gaol 'among felons and thieves'. Women were seldom segregated from the men and suffered as a result. One Newgate keeper was himself imprisoned for raping a female prisoner in 1449 and many similar cases must have gone undetected. Prisoners who could not afford to pay for a separate room were herded together.

Many prisoners died of starvation and thirst. Drinking water was often polluted. Even the well which supplied drinking water in the Tower of London was described as a place where 'the rats drown themselves'. But some unfortunates did not have a supply even of foul water. In the dungeons at Carlisle Castle the 'licking-stone' bears witness to this fact. This stone was grooved by the tongues of generations of prisoners who desperately tried to lick the moisture which dampened its surface. But too much water could be equally unpleasant. The feet of some prisoners actually rotted away from constantly resting in pools of stagnant water. Crowded, unventilated and insanitary, the prisons soon became a hotbed of disease. Cold and hunger also lowered prisoners' resistance. Many died of gaol-fever, a form of typhus.

Charitable Bequests

The desperate plight of prisoners was not totally ignored by officialdom. Exchequer grants and statutory provisions were made from time to time, but their scope was very limited. For example, a statute of 1283 only concerned debtors. By law, they were supposed to be supplied with bread and water by their creditors.

Royal donations were often made. In 1248, Henry III ordered alms to be distributed to all prisoners in Newgate on the first Monday in Lent. Sometimes prisoners were given goods seized as a result of a breach of the trade laws — for example, heads of animals confiscated at Norwich market in 1421, and fraudulently packed herrings in London in 1464. The church was among the more charitable of gaol owners. At the Archbishop of Canterbury's prison at Maidstone, each prisoner received one halfpenny per day during the later Middle Ages.

Prisoners also benefited from private gifts and bequests. Some bequests were very small, only a few pence. Others were more munificent: John of Gaunt left 100 marks (about £67) to two prisons while Sir Richard Whittington bequeathed £500 to four London prisons. Bequests were sometimes more specific. A London grocer, Robert Chichele, bequeathed money to supply every prisoner in certain London prisons with a halfpenny loaf per week for two

7 This picture from Froissart's *Chronicles* (late fourteenth century) shows how popular a public execution was. After confession, the prisoner waits for the axe to fall. Later, the body will be cut into four pieces and nailed to the city gates.

years. Other wills provided clothing, lights, beds and bedding, or faggots for a fire to stave off the winter's cold.

Such acts of mercy were, however, insufficient to meet all the prisoners' needs. Prisoners were sometimes allowed to beg through the barred windows of the gaol. In the 1370s, two of Colchester's aldermen set up two posts by the town gaol entrance where prisoners could be chained and allowed to beg from passers-by. Later on, in London, it was common to see prisoners from Ludgate gaol begging in the streets. In general, prisoners were far less isolated from the world outside than they are today. By the end of the thirteenth century, for example, debtors in the Fleet were allowed out, under escort, to attend to their business. Prisoners of rank were allowed considerable privileges. A knight, Jordon de Bianney, imprisoned during the reign of King John (1199-1216), was actually allowed to leave prison twice a day to engage in swordplay!

Prison Escapes

The numerous carvings which remain on prison walls today remind us how many prisoners whiled away the monotony of their incarceration. Most must have dreamed of escaping and some succeeded in doing so. The Tower of

London's first known prisoner was Ranulf Flambard, Bishop of Durham. His escape from the White Tower in the early twelfth century was also a 'first'. As befitted his rank, Flambard was allowed to send out for whatever he required and his imprisonment cannot have been too uncomfortable. One night, he wined and dined his guards to the point of stupefaction. He than managed to escape from one of the windows by sliding down a rope, taken from a wine jar, to the ground some 20 metres below. He had secretly arranged for his servants to meet him, and, with their help, managed to reach France and safety.

Escapes were also engineered by 'break-ins' from the outside. One October day in 1470, a crowd of about 300 stormed the Marshalsea and released 99 prisoners. Occasionally there were well-organized prison riots. Also during the fifteenth century, rioting prisoners climbed on to the prison roofs of Newgate and started hurling missiles at the sheriff and prison officials. In the end, the disturbance was crushed only with the help of a posse of local citizens.

It is not surprising that prisoners tried to escape or rioted. Some of them, it is true, were imprisoned because they could not pay the fine imposed on them by the courts and some because they could not pay their debts, but the overwhelming majority of prisoners were simply waiting to be brought to trial. People who had been arrested and cast into gaol, many of them on flimsy evidence, had to wait months or even years for their cases to be heard and sometimes were completely forgotten.

Gaol Delivery

The process by which all, or some, of the prisoners in a gaol were brought before the courts for trial and sentencing was known as gaol delivery. Gaols were supposed to be delivered, or cleared, twice a year. From the end of the thirteenth century, the judges usually allotted this task were the justices of assize, who tried the prisoners in the local prisons after they had held their assize sessions. They often delivered the local franchise gaols as well, and, eventually, although not without protest from some of the owners, all franchise gaols had to be regularly delivered.

Sometimes, when there was a backlog of cases waiting to be tried, special Commissions of Gaol Delivery were appointed to supplement the regular work done by the justices of assize. By the end of the fourteenth century, justices of the peace who had had legal training were allowed to serve on these commissions. At the same time, the sheriffs, who had long been associated in the public mind with crooked justice, were barred from such service. In their travels around the country, the king's justices were able to keep an eye on what was going on and to expose unfair practices. However, justice was by no means always done. One fourteenth-century poet rather bitterly commented: 'The lawful man shall be put in prison; the thief who ever does wrong shall escape.'

2
Troublous Times, 1500~1700

During the sixteenth and seventeenth centuries, England was torn by political and religious strife. In the ferment of ideas produced by the Reformation, religious fanaticism made political conflict all the more bitter. Constant rumours and intrigues fostered an atmosphere of fear and suspicion. In such a situation, the tendency was to throw suspects into prison on the flimsiest of evidence. Literally hundreds of people were held to await trial on political and religious charges. Most of these prisoners came from London and the south-east, and so it was principally to the London gaols that they were taken.

The Tower of London
The prison which has become the particular symbol of the repression and fear of the sixteenth century was the Tower of London. This was the chief prison of the realm for people who had committed offences against the state, and in this period it housed a most distinguished collection of prisoners.

Prisoners were generally taken to the Tower of London via the Traitors' Gate beneath St Thomas's Tower by a concealed entrance from the River Thames. The mere fact of being brought in by the Traitors' Gate was in itself gloomily suggestive, and when as a young princess the future Queen Elizabeth I was taken to the Tower she is said to have protested vehemently against being delivered there as if she were a traitor. Important prisoners would then have been taken to their quarters in one of the towers in the outer wall.

Some of the towers became associated with a certain class of prisoner. Thus, the Salt Tower was the place to which religious prisoners were often sent. Many Jesuits were held there at one time or another. It also housed persons accused of witchcraft, after this was declared a crime in 1541. One of them, Hew Draper, accused of witchcraft against Bess of Hardwick, in 1561 carved a figure for casting horoscopes on the wall of the tower.

Countless prisoners in their time were lodged in the Beauchamp Tower, leaving their memorials in the many carvings on the walls. Above the fireplace there is an inscription: 'The more suffering for Christ in this world the more Glory with Christ in the next.' This was written by Philip Howard, Earl of Arundel, in 1587. Lady Jane Grey's husband, Guildford Dudley, is thought to have been the author of the simple inscription 'Iane'. Sometimes carvings were unsigned and undated, like this one: 'Close prisoner 8 months, 32 wekes, 224 dayes, 5376 houres' — time could pass slowly in prison.

Prisoners of wealth and rank would have been accorded a degree of comfort befitting their position. They were allowed to send out for most of what they required. Traditionally, their gaolers would have been open to bribes and, in any case, some may have been not unsympathetic towards their distinguished charges.

The majority of prisoners, however, awaited their fate with a mixture of hope and fear, of resignation and despair. Whatever care prisoners took in preparing their defence, most must have known that the outcome of their trial would be a mere formality. It was difficult to know, too, how far anyone was to be trusted. A letter written by the Princess Elizabeth (suspected of being involved in Sir Thomas Wyatt's rebellion of 1554) to her sister Mary Tudor shows just how careful she had to be. Elizabeth vigorously denied the charges, begging 'that I be not condemned without answer and due proof, which it seems that I now am'. The letter did not extend quite to two full pages, and so Elizabeth scored diagonal lines with her pen across the unused portion of the last page. In this way she hoped to prevent anyone from tampering with it after it left her hands.

8 An eighteenth century print of Tower Hill. The last execution at this famous spot took place in 1747.

Public Executions

Prisoners of high rank who were found guilty of treason were at least granted the privilege of being executed. They were thus spared the lingering death of ordinary traitors, who were hanged, drawn and quartered before the assembled crowds at Tyburn, where Marble Arch now stands. However, even high-ranking prisoners had to face the ordeal of living within sight or earshot of their place of execution. Lady Jane Grey, from her prison window, could see the headless body of her husband brought back from Tower Hill, and listen to the blows of the hammers as her own scaffold was being made ready.

But when the time came, death traditionally brought forth an incredible display of courage and fortitude. The crowds who massed to hear the victim's death oration were seldom disappointed. But it is perhaps more in his private last words that the true poignancy of the condemned man's plight is conveyed. Below there is an extract from a letter Sir Walter Ralegh wrote to his wife in December 1603, on the night before his execution was due to take place, not knowing that James I would order a last-minute reprieve:

You shall receave, deare wife, my last words in these my last lynes. My love I send you, that you may keepe it when I am dead; and my councell, that you may remember it when I am noe more. I would not, with my last Will, present you with sorrowes, deare Besse. Lett them goe to the grave with me, and be buried in the dust. And, seeing it is not the will of God that ever I shall see you in this life, beare my destruccion gentlie . . . God knowes how hardlie I stole this tyme, when all sleep; and it is tyme to separate my thoughts from the world. Begg my dead body, which living was denyed you . . . I can wright noe more. Tyme and death call me awaye.

9 This seventeenth century print shows some of the men responsible for the execution of Charles I themselves being hanged, drawn and quartered. The crowd cheered when the head and heart of one of the culprits was held aloft.

The use of torture, already widespread in Europe, increased in England during the sixteenth century. The Renaissance was, after all, a cruel and ruthless period as well as a time in which the arts and sciences flourished and men discovered new worlds. In England, plots and political intrigues encouraged its use.

Stubborn prisoners were often taken to the torture chamber under the White Tower for 'questioning'. Here, Father Gerard was brought from the Salt Tower, where he was imprisoned in the 1590s, and suspended by manacles attached to his wrists. In fact, much of the equipment of any ordinary gaol — manacles, fetters and so on — could be used as weapons of torture. In addition, there were instruments specially designed for the purpose. The best known of these was the rack or brake on which prisoners' limbs were stretched. According to Sir Edward Coke, Chief Justice in the reigns of Elizabeth I and James I, the rack was introduced by John Holland, first Duke of Exeter and Constable of the Tower under Henry VI (1422-71). With a macabre kind of humour, it was nicknamed 'the Duke of Exeter's daughter'.

Another common method of torture was the *peine forte et dure* (literally 'severe and hard punishment'). In the Middle Ages, it was used to force prisoners to plead either guilty or not guilty to the charges laid against them, for if a prisoner refused to plead, his trial could not proceed. In practice, it meant that the prisoner was thrown into a dungeon and fed, on alternate days, with a morsel of bread and a little water. By the fifteenth century, the *peine forte et dure* had come to mean not simply rigorous imprisonment but severe pain. It became customary to place enormously heavy weights upon the prisoner, with the result that the unfortunate victim was sometimes literally crushed to death. In the sixteenth century, this torture was applied increasingly to force religious prisoners to recant, or to reveal information.

During the persecution of the Protestants in Mary Tudor's reign (1553-8), many religious offenders were taken to Newgate Gaol to await a martyr's death on the funeral pyre at nearby Smithfield. Much of what we know about the ill-treatment of religious prisoners at this time is provided by John Foxe. In his *Book of Martyrs*, published in 1562-3, Foxe spared his readers none of the gory details. The book became a bestseller of the period, probably second only to the Bible, and did much to inflame anti-Catholic feeling.

According to Foxe, the keeper of Newgate, Andrew Alexander, bore a special hatred for his Protestant prisoners. His only desire was to get them to the stake as quickly as possible. Alexander's methods of dealing with his prisoners is illustrated by his treatment of John Philpot, Archdeacon of Winchester. The keeper promised to show him 'every pleasure' if he would recant. When the Archdeacon refused, Alexander 'commanded him to be set upon the block with as many irons upon his legs as he could bear'. When Philpot cried for mercy, Alexander is reported to have replied: 'Give me my fees and I will take them off; if not, thou shalt wear them still'. But when Philpot offered him all the money he had with him he sneered, 'What is that to me?' Finally, the Archdeacon was cast into a dungeon where, says Foxe, 'he died miserably, being so swollen that he was more like a monster than a man.'

10 A torture chamber. A secretary waits, quill-pen in hand, to take down incriminating evidence wrung from the prisoner.

11 A woodcut showing a heretic being burned at the stake. This was a common fate shared by both Protestant and Catholic prisoners who refused to give up or change their faith in the sixteenth century.

12 An old village lock-up, Dorset. Vagrants rounded up by the parish constable were held in the local lock-up until they could be brought before the justices of the peace.

Corrupt though many gaolers undoubtedly were, their work was not made any easier by the increasing number of prisoners they were expected to cram into their gaols. The sheer pressure of numbers was felt to some extent in all the larger towns, but particularly in London. Although it was still just an overgrown medieval town rather than a modern metropolis, relatively speaking London suffered from the same growing pains as any rapidly emerging city today. As it became more prosperous, it offered easier pickings for the thief and down-and-out. As it became more crowded, it afforded a cloak of anonymity to the rogue, who could protect himself from detection by mingling with the jostling crowds in the narrow streets and alleys.

With the crumbling of the old feudal order of society many people were thrown out of work. The large military retinues which the great households in medieval times had employed for protection and the waging of private wars were gradually disbanded. Peasants, too, were dispossessed as the thriving wool industry encouraged pastoral at the expense of arable farming. Some drifted to the towns while others squatted where they could on common land on the village outskirts.

After Henry VIII's dissolution of the monasteries in the 1530s, the monastic estates were streamlined under their new lay owners, and many of the former retainers — the bakers, the launderers, the gardeners and so on — were made redundant.

Perhaps the most unruly of all the vagrants were the discharged soldiers and sailors. After the failure of the Norris and Drake expedition to Portugal in 1589, the disbanded servicemen drifted up to London and threatened to loot Bartholomew Fair. So grave was the crisis that 2,000 City militia men were called out to deal with it.

In addition there were the genuine nomads, the gypsies, who first began to appear in England in the sixteenth century. 'The wretched, wily, wandering vagabonds calling and naming themselves Egyptians' were soon regarded as a major menace by local justices of the peace.

Among vagrants in general there was a new and disturbing element — the professional criminal. These people were masters in the art of the confidence trick, of low cunning and deceit. In his *Description of England* (1587), William Harrison listed 14 different types of male rogues — rufflers, uprightmen, hookers or anglers, drunken tinkers, among others. Female rogues were called 'morts'. Among them were to be found demanders for glimmer (that is, beggars claiming to have lost everything in a fire), bawdy-baskets and doxies. These Elizabethan drop-outs created a world of their own and spoke their own particular kind of slang.

Writers were fascinated by the new criminal underworld. Robert Greene explained the jargon of the 'cony-catcher' or cheat in a book published in 1591. For example, stolen goods were 'garbage' and the receiver of them the 'marker'. Horse-stealing, probably as common then as car-stealing today, was 'prigging'. The horse-stealer was the 'prigger', and the horse he stole the 'prancer'.

13 The pillory, like the stocks, was a form of punishment by humiliation. Missiles and abuse were hurled at the culprits by jeering spectators.

The House of Correction, or Bridewell

London's answer to the problem of vagrancy was the House of Correction or Bridewell. There, 'the vagabond and ydle strumpet' were to be 'chastised and compelled to labour'. The first House of Correction was the former royal palace of Bridewell, handed over for the purpose to the City of London by Edward VI in 1553. A statute of 1576 provided that more bridewells should be set up elsewhere in the country. In 1609, the justices of the peace were made directly responsible for them.

The bridewells were not intended to be prisons. Rather, they were workhouses for able-bodied, unemployed tramps who had not as yet committed an offence. Unlike the gaols, the houses of correction were supposed to be financed as far as possible by the work of the inmates. In 1579, among the 25 different trades practised at the London Bridewell were the making of pins, lace, gloves, silk and even tennis balls.

The bridewell regime was, however, prison-like. Sentences were often long — as much as five years at Winchester, for example. Labour was compulsory and was enforced by rigid discipline, usually whipping. Unruly inmates could also be placed in irons or have their sentences arbitrarily extended.

The houses of correction appeared at first to achieve their objective. Sir Edward Coke commented: 'Few or none are committed to the common gaole . . . but they come out worse than they went in. And few are committed to the house of correction . . . but they come out better.' But this was not to last long. By 1720, justices of the peace were authorized to commit minor offenders to a house of correction. From then onwards, minor criminals were sent there in increasing numbers. Soon the only difference between a gaol and a house of correction was that, in the latter, forced labour was practised. In time, they became plagued with the same abuses already rife in the prisons.

14 The prison-like entrance of the House of Correction, Middlesex (nineteenth century print.

Attempts at Reform

During the sixteenth and seventeenth centuries, some attempts were made by Parliament to improve prison conditions. The responsibility for seeing that such measures were carried out was entrusted to the justices of the peace, but they were generally not over-zealous in carrying out their duties.

In 1572, justices of the peace were required to levy a small parish rate for bread to be distributed to destitute prisoners convicted of serious crimes. This was the County Allowance. The Act only applied to the county gaols, however, and debtors, minor offenders and untried prisoners were not entitled to receive the allowance. Despite its limitations, the Act was an important landmark. It was the first time that Parliament had made it clear that the authorities at local level should contribute towards the upkeep of some of their prisoners.

A permanent grievance of prisoners was the unbearable length of time they were forced to wait in gaol before they were tried. To prevent this, Parliament in 1679 passed the Habeas Corpus Act. *Habeas Corpus* in Latin literally means 'you may have the body'. By the act, a writ of Habeas Corpus could be issued

15 Many poor prisoners would have starved to death but for charity (sixteenth century woodcut).

to a gaoler ordering him to produce his prisoner for trial at a specific time and place. Delays continued, but the act had at least established an offender's right to be heard within a reasonable space of time.

For the most part, however, the improvement of prison conditions depended solely upon the goodwill of county, municipal or private owners of gaols. Some civic authorities made a show of concern. The Aldermen of the City of London, for instance, became worried about the spiritual welfare of prisoners. From 1544, visiting chaplains were appointed to Newgate. They were called Ordinaries or Visitors of Newgate. One of their duties was to compile case-histories of notorious prisoners. Collections of these, under the title *The Newgate Calendar*, were published at the beginning of the nineteenth century.

A new interest was shown in prisoners' health. Personal cleanliness was virtually impossible when, as one prisoner put it, lice were 'their most common companion'. But lice were a triviality compared with other health risks. Far more dangerous were the polluted drinking-water, the primitive sanitation and the cramming together of the healthy with the sick and dying. Outbreaks of gaol-fever recurred frequently. In 1674, a Dr Hodges was paid 'to inform himself of the gravity of the distemper of the prisoners in Wood Street Compter' (one of the London gaols). Records of moneys paid to apothecaries show that some medicines were purchased to treat sick prisoners. Sometimes one reads of 'diseased prisoners' being separated from the rest. Concern was also shown from time to time about Newgate's water supply and about the cleansing of the prison. Generally speaking, all these efforts only touched on the fringes of the problem and did nothing to solve it. Probably the most cleansing measure, although shortlived in its effects, was fire.

John Evelyn the diarist was in London when the Great Fire started in Pudding Lane, early on the morning of 2 September 1666. On 4 September Evelyn wrote that 'all Fleet Street, Ludgate Hill, Warwick Lane, Newgate and the Old Bailey was now flaming and most of it reduced to ashes'. Unfortunately, little is known about the fate of the prisoners, or how complete was the destruction of Newgate. But, however good the intentions of the Committee for Rebuilding the Sessions House and the Gaol of Newgate, appointed in 1666, may have been, the new prison soon became as bad as the old.

Alternative Punishments

The idea that prisoners should be forced to render some useful service to the country was not a new one. For some time, selected prisoners had been removed from gaol and drafted into the army or navy. Prison authorities were only too glad to get rid of some of their prisoners. In 1619, the Lord Mayor of London reported to James I that Newgate held men well suited 'for service in foreign parts'. In the summer of 1623, a list of suitable recruits was submitted with the comment: 'They pester the gaol this hot weather, and would do better service as soldiers than if pardoned, for they would not dare to run away.'

In 1577, 'condemned men' were recruited for Frobisher's second voyage in search of the North-West Passage to China and the East. Although they did not in the end take part in the expedition, the idea that convicts might be helpful overseas took root. A number of prisoners were sent out to Virginia after the settlement was founded in 1607. In 1615, it was ordered that those found guilty of 'anie robberie or fellonie (wilfull murther, rape, witchcraft or burglarie only excepted)' should be despatched overseas. It was hoped that the prisoners 'might be rather corrected than destroyed and that . . . some may live and yeald a profitable service to the commonwealthe in partes abroad'. Later on in the century, it was enacted that people convicted of certain offences might be pardoned if they agreed to be deported to the colonies.

By no means all of those who were transported were criminals. It was soon realized that the colonies provided an admirable place to which religious and political undesirables might be sent. Between 1655 and 1699 a total of 4,500 prisoners of various kinds had been sent to America and the West Indies. Although some made good, they were generally despised and very harshly treated. The more self-righteous citizens of Barbados protested in 1654 that 'this Iland is the Dunghill whereon England doth cast forth its rubidg'.

3
Eighteenth-century Prisons

'Fashionable' Prisons

In the eighteenth century, Newgate was easily the most notorious prison in the whole of England. It was a major attraction not only for the Londoners themselves, but also for visitors from other parts of the country and overseas. Those who wanted to go inside and look at the unfortunate prisoners were admitted on the payment of a fee to the gaoler.

Writers and artists recorded their impressions of the experience. James Boswell (1740-95) went there on his very first visit to London and on the following day attended a hanging. The artist William Hogarth was also a frequent visitor to Newgate, for the gaol provided him with models for his work. Two days before she was hanged, Hogarth drew the portrait of Sarah Malcolm, who had been convicted of three vicious murders. The expression on her face, he said, showed her to be 'capable of any wickedness'.

It was from Newgate that convicted prisoners were taken in open procession to face their public execution on the gallows at Tyburn Hill. The darling of the crowds who thronged the streets on the day of execution was the highwayman, immortalized in John Gay's *The Beggar's Opera*, which enjoyed a phenomenal success when it was first performed at the Theatre Royal in 1728. Hero-worship of highwaymen became a kind of cult in the early eighteenth century. One of the more colourful personalities was Jack Rann. He once appeared in court before the magistrate Sir John Fielding sporting a bunch of flowers in his coat and with his irons decorated with blue ribbons! He was popularly known as Sixteen-String Jack, because he habitually wore eight different coloured strings on each leg of his knee-breeches. Women were fascinated by him and he was found entertaining a number of his admirers at dinner at Newgate the night before his execution.

Another highwayman, Jack Sheppard, became famous for his daring escapes from Newgate. Sheppard was finally brought to book at Tyburn in 1724. An adoring crowd showered him with flowers as he made his journey by cart to the gallows. Six months later, the same crowd turned out to pelt Jonathan Wild with mud and stones as he wended his way to Tyburn, for it was Wild who had given information leading to Sheppard's arrest.

16 People rushed to their windows and thronged the streets to cheer or revile the condemned man on his way to Tyburn.

17 Newgate gaol (c. 1895). Rebuilt several times during its long history, Newgate was finally demolished at the beginning of the twentieth century.

Conditions in Newgate

The practice which medieval gaolers had adopted of making prisoners pay for their board and lodging had eventually led to the division of even quite small gaols into two well-defined areas: the master's side (for the well-to-do offender) and the common side (for the poor). Rather as hotels today charge more for rooms with a good view or a private bathroom, so the eighteenth-century gaoler offered his 'guests' accommodation of varying degrees of comfort — and of cost.

As one of London's larger gaols, Newgate was able to offer a variety of accommodation which the smaller provincial gaols of the period could not possibly have provided. On both sides of the gaol, separate accommodation was provided for men and women, but there was no special provision for juvenile offenders or for untried prisoners. Prisoners condemned to death were placed in a special condemned 'hold', one for men and one for women. In principle debtors were kept apart from criminal offenders, but in practice they mixed together a good deal during the daytime.

On the common side of Newgate, there were three male criminal wards and two for women. Female debtors, if any, had to be placed in the criminal wards, but there were four male debtor wards. All necessities, including beds, had to be paid for. However, debtors received a free daily ration of bread and a little beef once a week. Other offenders also benefited from charity. Criminals who could pay the required 'civility money' of one shilling (5p.) could enjoy the comparative cleanliness and tidiness of the best male criminal ward, Middle Ward. Those who were penniless were liable to be relegated to the worst criminal ward, Stone Hold. Prisoners there had nothing to sleep on but the cold, stone-paved floor.

On the master's side, there were several wards for debtors and criminals. The most affluent criminals would probably have opted to stay in the Press Yard, the most comfortable of the criminal wards. There, the rooms were 'large and spacious' and 'well supplied with light and air, free from smells and well equipped'. Domestic help could be hired, visitors could come and go almost as they pleased, and exercise could be taken out of doors. With nothing to do, prisoners seem to have spent most of their time gossiping, drinking and gambling. Indeed, the Press Yard at night-time was said to have been 'like the tap-room of a common inn'.

Religious services in Newgate were held on the third floor, in the Chapel. Prisoners from the master's and common sides were seated separately from one another. Church attendance was optional, except for condemned prisoners, who were obliged to receive Holy Communion on the day before their execution. Prisoners were not among the most devout of congregations. Chapel services were usually noisy and riotous affairs.

The extent to which torture was used depended very much on the individual gaoler. Certainly, the equipment was still there. At Newgate, there was a group of sinister rooms. One was called Bilbows. This was where prisoners of either

19 By the eighteenth century, it was common practice for the prisoner community to demand garnish — a kind of entrance fee — from all newly-arrived prisoners. The rule was 'Strip or pay'. This man was about to lose his coat because he cannot pay the required fee.

18 Prisoners — probably debtors — being transferred from New Prison Clerkenwell to Newgate pause for refreshments at an inn (late eighteenth century).

20 Eighteenth century methods of hanging were not always foolproof. John Smith's miraculous recovery after he was cut down from the gallows earned him the nick-name 'Half-hanged Smith' and a mention in the Newgate Calendar.

sex could be forcibly taken and flogged, or put in irons. Prisoners who refused to plead at the Old Bailey, the famous criminal court which served the prison, might be taken to the Press Room, where they were pressed by heavy weights — the *peine forte et dure*. One of Newgate's more repellent 'chambers of horrors' was Jack Ketch's Kitchen, named after the public executioner in the time of Charles II. This was where the dismembered corpses of persons executed for treason were disposed of.

The Prison Community

Entering prison for the first time must have been a frightening experience. Daniel Defoe, who spent six months as a prisoner in Newgate in 1703, many years later wrote a book, *Moll Flanders* (1722), based on his experiences. Caught stealing some silk brocade, Moll is imprisoned in Newgate to await trial: "'Tis impossible to describe the terror of my mind, when I was first brought in . . . the hellish noise, the roaring, swearing and clamour, the stench and nastiness, and all the dreadful afflicting things that I saw there, joined to make the place seem an emblem of hell itself.' After the initial shock, the horrors of the place became familiar and Moll found herself behaving just like the 'hell-hounds' around her. 'In a word', she says, 'I was become a mere Newgate-bird, as wicked and as outrageous as any of them.'

The prison community devised its own rules of conduct. Every new prisoner had to go through the initiation of paying *garnish*, which in many cases meant that they were robbed of everything of value they possessed, down to the very clothes on their backs. A Jacobite who was imprisoned in Newgate after the Jacobite rising of 1715 wrote a book called *The History of the Press Yard* in which he described how garnish was collected on the master's side. A fellow prisoner explained the system to him: 'You will, according to custom, about seven or eight of the clock this evening be called upon to pay your entrance fee.' The fee was 'formerly only six bottles of wine, and tobacco in proportion, but it is now raised to ten or twelve'. Prisoners who did not have enough money were allowed credit.

The Jacobite's initiatory evening was spent in good-humoured revelry. He found himself constantly 'whipping out sixpences to advance more bottles' for his 'immensely civil' companions. Eventually, those who were still sober went up to their rooms, 'the turnkeys locking each of the two staircase doors after us'. Next morning, all those who had been drunk on the previous night were brought before a mock court presided over by the turnkeys, and forfeits in the form of wine and spirits were exacted from them.

Poverty and Punishment

Most of the prisoners committed to gaol to await trial were not professional criminals like Jack Rann or Jack Sheppard nor were they evil characters such as Sarah Malcolm was said to be. The majority were simply ordinary people who were driven to commit petty offences because they were cold and hungry and unemployed.

Poverty was everywhere, but most of all in London. The novelist and London magistrate, Henry Fielding (1707-54), was shocked by the immorality of London's poor, but moved to compassion by the wretched conditions in which they eked out their miserable existence. Some families had only a single loaf of bread to last them the entire week. 'If any of these creatures falls sick (and it is almost a miracle that stench, vermin and want should ever suffer them to be well) they are turned out into the street.' The streets teemed with beggars.

Since such privation and misery existed outside the gaols, it was not surprising that the plight of prisoners provoked little concern. The filthy conditions of gaols might have received more attention if standards of cleanliness had been high elsewhere. But despite improvements in public sanitation, even the streets were dirty and smelly. Similarly, if savage corporal punishment in prisons and the use of torture went largely without comment, it was because ideas on discipline in general were so harsh. Punishments in the armed forces were notoriously brutal, but such severity was justified on the grounds that order had to be maintained. The same sort of attitude existed towards crime. If more crimes were being committed, the only answer the authorities could see was to make punishments tougher. When George II ascended the throne in 1727, there were about 50 capital offences. By 1770, the number had grown to 160 and continued to rise. Of course, such a policy was self-defeating. Punishments became so severe that they ceased to have any meaning for the criminal, who began to feel that he might just as well be hanged for a sheep as for a lamb. Furthermore, the courts became reluctant to impose the death sentence and many prisoners were transported instead. But there remained a good deal of public indignation against the prevalence of crime; although people might not like to send a man to his death, they had little sympathy to spare for the criminal once he had been imprisoned.

In view of all this, it is hardly surprising to find that there were few who pressed for prison reforms or an improvement in the treatment of prisoners in the first half of the eighteenth century. The only major steps towards reform were taken, quite by chance, at the insistence of the Member of Parliament for Haslemere, General James Oglethorpe (1696 - 1785).

London's Debtor Prisons

A very large proportion of the country's prison population was made up of debtors. Many of them had been imprisoned for the non-payment of trifling sums. The ease with which payment by instalments could be made was then, as now, a trap for the unwary. As soon as they failed to pay, they were liable to be taken to court. Once sent to prison, the unfortunate debtor would

21 The despair and degradation of a debtor and his family imprisoned in the Fleet, portrayed by William Hogarth in *A Rake's Progress* (1735).

flounder more deeply into debt because of the extortionate demands made upon him by the gaoler and his assistants.

It was the tragic case of a personal friend, Robert Castell, which goaded General Oglethorpe into action. Castell had had the misfortune to be committed to the Fleet Prison when Thomas Bambridge was the warden. Bambridge used to offer debtors accommodation in one of his private lodgings for debtors — or 'spunging-houses' as they were called. This was a subtle form of blackmail, for the prisoner would willingly risk running into further debt to pay the exorbitant rent demanded rather than face the horrors of the ordinary gaol. When Castell's money was nearly exhausted, Bambridge threatened to send him to another spunging-house in the Fleet where smallpox had broken out. Castell had never had smallpox, and was terrified of catching it. Bambridge ignored his pleas and moved him, whereupon Castell contracted the disease and died. Oglethorpe had visited his friend in prison. Horrified by what he had seen, he decided to raise the matter in Parliament.

In 1729, the House of Commons appointed a special committee, chaired by Oglethorpe, to look into the matter. The committee's report on the Fleet was presented in March of the same year. It appeared that Bambridge and a colleague had purchased the wardenship of the Fleet from the then warden, John Huggins, for £5,000 — an enormous sum in those days. No proper accounts were kept by Bambridge, but the committee was assured that the Christmas donations of prisoners amounted alone to more than £2,800. No record had been kept of prisoners admitted to the gaol nor of exactly where they were lodged. In this respect, Huggins appeared to have been as lax as Bambridge, for he admitted that 'so many prisoners had escaped during his time as warden that it was impossible to enumerate them, he having kept no list of the persons so escaped'.

A dungeon called the Strong Room was used by Bambridge as a place of punishment. The committee reported: 'This place is a vault, like those in which the dead are interred, and wherein the bodies of persons dying in the said prison are usually deposited till the coroner's inquest hath passed upon them.' Made of rough, unplastered brick, the Strong Room had no light except 'what comes over the door', no chimney and no fireplace. 'What adds to the dampness and stench of the place is its being built over the common shore, and adjoining to the sink and dunghill where all the nastiness of the prison is cast.' Many acts of cruelty were brought to light. The committee recommended that Bambridge, Huggins and four prison officials should be committed to Newgate and prosecuted for their misdeeds.

The Oglethorpe Committee's second report, submitted in May 1729, concerned the Marshalsea Prison. The prison was supposed to be in the care of the Deputy Marshal, but early in 1727 he had leased it to a butcher by the name of William Acton. The lease and rent cost Acton £400 per year. To recoup this expenditure, and make a profit as well, Acton oppressed his prisoners unmercifully.

The Marshalsea was found to be rife with the same abuses as the Fleet. The wards were fearfully overcrowded and, on occasion, dead bodies were left lying in the rooms alongside the living. Implements of torture included the thumbscrew and an iron collar. Some victims had been so tightly constricted by the collar that they had suffocated to death. It was recommended that proceedings be taken against Acton and his associates.

The King's Bench Prison was the next to be investigated. Rents and fees were once again a target of criticism, but, unlike Bambridge and Acton, the keeper of the King's Bench Prison seems to have been a man of some compassion and thus earned the committee's commendation.

Official Action

Bambridge and Huggins were eventually tried at the Old Bailey for murdering various prisoners in the Fleet. Both were acquitted. Tried at Surrey Assizes on similar charges, Acton, too, was acquitted. The outcome of these trials shows how difficult it was to bring people in such positions to justice, despite the evidence against them.

As a result of the Oglethorpe Committee investigations, in 1729 Parliament passed the Insolvent Debtors' Relief Act. The act abolished the spunging-houses and obliged creditors to contribute towards the upkeep of their imprisoned debtors. But the law was ignored and 30 years later the plight of debtors was still as bad. Yet another act was passed. This time Quarter Sessions were required to draw up rules and regulations 'for the better government of their respective gaols'. Once approved by the judges of assize, the rules were supposed to be forwarded to the keepers who were to hang them up 'in some public room' in their gaols.

The responsibility for implementing these reforms clearly lay with the local Quarter Sessions, for the Home Secretary had no power to enforce the laws. On the whole, however, judges remained apathetic. Their marked reluctance to visit gaols and houses of correction was not without reason, for the gaol-fever prevalent there was highly infectious. Even without setting foot in a gaol it was easy enough to contract the dreaded disease. The October sessions at the Old Bailey in 1750 went down in history as the 'Black Sessions'. On that occasion, 'the foul steams of the Bail Dock, and of two rooms opening into the Court in which the prisoners were the whole day crowded together' had been particularly noticeable. Nearly everyone in court was taken ill and the death toll of 40 included four out of the six judges on the bench. If systematic gaol inspection was to be carried out, it was obvious that much courage and determination were required.

22 A trial at the Old Bailey, London's famous Criminal Court, depicted by Thomas Rowlandson and A. C. Pugin (1808).

4

The Age of Enlightenment

John Howard (1726-90)

The much-needed inquiry into the state of the prisons had to wait until the second half of the eighteenth century, in particular for a very determined and courageous campaigner: John Howard. John Howard was born in Hackney, London, in 1726. His mother died soon after his birth, and he was brought up by his father in Bedfordshire. When Howard was 16 his father also died, leaving him comfortably off so that he had no need to work for a living.

Despite his fortune, Howard was a man of very simple tastes, with an extraordinary sense of duty towards his fellow men. Perhaps his only self-indulgence and lifelong passion was his love of travel. Hearing that there had been an earthquake in Lisbon, he decided to go there to help in whatever way he could. He set off in 1756 aboard the *Hanover*. War meanwhile had broken out between England and France and, before Howard's ship could reach Portugal, it was captured by a French privateer and taken to Brest. This marked a turning point in Howard's life, for it was as a prisoner of war that he gained first-hand experience of what it was like to be imprisoned. When he was eventually allowed to return to England on parole, he made a point of reporting the sufferings of his fellow-prisoners, still languishing in a French gaol, and in so doing helped to secure their release.

Howard was to be unlucky in his private life. By the age of 39, he had twice been a widower and his only son was mentally handicapped. Howard assuaged his sorrows by devoting himself to the care of his estate in Bedfordshire. He was a model landlord, building schools for his tenants' children and cottages on his land for poor and homeless families.

In 1773, he was appointed High Sheriff of Bedfordshire. Soon Howard had amazed everyone by taking his duties seriously. Officially the sheriffs were still responsible for the county gaols, but it was many years since any sheriff had looked upon this as more than a formality. Consequently, when Howard decided to carry out a thorough inspection of Bedford Gaol, people thought he had taken leave of his senses.

What Howard saw convinced him that reform was long overdue. Most of the evils seemed to him to stem from the fact that the gaoler was allowed to run his

23 John Howard: Prison Reformer (1726-1790) (from an engraving by T. Holloway).

37

prison as a personal profit-making concern. Accordingly, he proposed that all fees should be abolished, that the gaoler should be paid a fixed salary and that the gaol should come under the direct administration of Quarter Sessions.

The justices made sympathetic noises when confronted with his proposals, but they said they could not possibly suggest charging the county with the cost of these reforms unless Howard could point to another authority which had adopted these ideas. No doubt the judges imagined the matter would rest there, but they had reckoned without Howard's single-mindedness and tenacity of purpose.

'I therefore rode', he said, 'into several neighbouring counties in search of one, but I soon learned that the same injustice was practised in them, and looking into the prisons, beheld scenes of calamity which I grew daily more and more anxious to alleviate.'

Those words formed part of the opening pages of Howard's report *State of the Prisons*, which was published in 1777. Nowadays the collection of data by one fact-finding commission or another is commonplace, and it is difficult for us to understand just how original Howard's survey seemed at the time. Not only was every detail precisely and accurately recorded — even down to the exact measurements of each cell and the size and number of its windows — but all was related in a dry, unsentimental, matter-of-fact manner.

By the end of 1774, Howard had journeyed all over the country visiting prisons and houses of correction. Not content with a 'one-off' survey, he continued his travels over the next 16 years revisiting gaols he had already inspected and extending his area of research to include Western Europe, Sweden and Russia. The Methodist leader John Wesley called him 'one of the greatest men in Europe', and in his lifetime he acquired an international reputation.

Without private means, Howard could not possibly have done what he did. Every penny he spent on his work came out of his own pocket. But far more important than his financial resources were his enormous reserves of courage and persistence. Prison visiting was a dangerous and unpleasant occupation. In his book Howard described some of the hazards:

It was not, I own, without some apprehensions of danger that I first visited the prisons: and I guarded myself by smelling vinegar while I was in these places, and changing my apparel afterwards. . . My clothes were in my first journeys so offensive that in a post-chaise I could not bear the windows drawn up; and was therefore obliged to travel commonly on horseback. The leaves of my memorandum book were often so tainted that I could not use it till after spreading it an hour or two before the fire. . . I do not wonder that in those journeys many gaolers made excuses and did not want to go with me into the felons' wards.

Howard's travels took him to 518 prisons in England and Wales. But such a large number of institutions contained a relatively small number of prisoners — a total of 4,375, according to his estimate of 1779. Nearly half of them were debtors. The rest were prisoners awaiting trial for major and minor offences, those already tried but waiting to serve a sentence of transportation and, finally, those who had been committed to prison for failure to find sureties for bail. Only the London prisons housed more than 90 prisoners at a time — the largest was the King's Bench Prison which contained 498 prisoners in 1779, all of them debtors. Outside the London area, only seven county gaols accommodated 50 or more prisoners and in 130 gaols and houses of correction, the number was less than ten.

Many of the prisons Howard visited might have come straight out of the Middle Ages. In York and Lancaster, part of a castle was still being used as a prison. At Kidderminster, two or three dark 'dungeons' under the market or court-house served a similar purpose. In all the gaols he visited, whether county, municipal or privately-owned, Howard found the same kind of abuses which Oglethorpe had uncovered so many years ago in the London gaols.

From the outset, Howard's activities aroused considerable interest. In 1774, Alexander Popham, M.P. for Taunton, asked him to give evidence in support of some reforms he was trying to get through Parliament. Howard's sincerity and forceful testimony were so impressive that enough support was won to carry Popham's Bills. The first act abolished discharge fees and provided that persons acquitted or discharged should be set at liberty in open court. They were not to be returned to prison simply because of debts incurred while awaiting trial. The second act 'authorized and required' justices of the peace 'to order the walls and ceilings of the several cells and wards . . . to be scraped and whitewashed once in the year at least'. This last measure would, it was hoped, check the spread of disease. Depressingly little resulted from this legislation. Some years later, Howard found that the law had been strictly obeyed in only 15 out of 150 prisons.

Howard's Four Principles

When he had given evidence in favour of Popham's proposals, Howard had put forward four basic recommendations which he considered fundamental to proper prison administration. Firstly, the building should be secure, roomy and sanitary. Secondly, the gaoler should be a salaried employee, subject to a public authority. Thirdly, the prisoners should be properly fed, supplied with work and encouraged in religious worship. Fourthly, the gaols should be systematically inspected by some outside public authority. Howard was never in favour of complete solitary confinement, although he did recommend separate sleeping quarters for each prisoner.

Howard's continuous investigations made prisons a talking-point, and his suggestions for their reform stimulated discussion among leading public figures.

The Utilitarians

One of Howard's admirers was Jeremy Bentham (1748-1832). Called to the Bar in 1772, Bentham soon established an international reputation as a writer on law and political economy and became the leading light among a group of philosophical radicals known as the Utilitarians. Bentham produced his own blueprint of the ideal prison, which he called the Panopticon. Around the perimeter of a vast, circular building, a number of individual cells were to be constructed, in which each convict was to be separately confined. The cells were designed so that the convicts could be under the constant surveillance of the prison inspector or warder, whose quarters were situated at the centre of the Panopticon.

Bentham had no intention of making imprisonment a pleasurable experience. He suggested that every prison gate should bear the notice: 'Had they been industrious when free, they need not have drudged here like slaves.' Although Bentham's Panopticon was too impractical to be implemented as it stood, some of his ideas were eventually incorporated into the planning of the model penitentiary at Millbank in London which was built some years later.

24 A portrait of Jeremy Bentham (1748-1832), painted by Worthington.

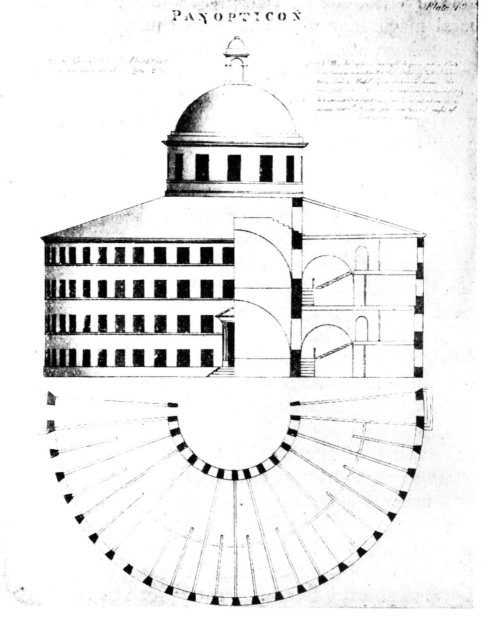

PANOPTICON

25 The Panopticon or Inspection House: Jeremy Bentham's idea for a model prison, published in 1791. Although Bentham secured a contract in 1794 with the Treasury to build a Panopticon and a site was acquired, nothing came of the project.

26 Convicts from the hulks at work raising ballast from the River Thames and building an embankment at Woolwich (London Magazine, 1777). The convicts were kept in leg irons all the time, even at night. Some were chained together in pairs.

While Howard concentrated on the practical, day-to-day problems of prisoners' welfare and prison management, the Utilitarians were more concerned with the broader philosophical questions of what caused people to commit crimes in the first place and of how society could best curb such anti-social activities. It was largely as a result of the persuasive arguments of Bentham and his followers that criminal law was reformed in the first half of the nineteenth century.

Prison Hulks

Another factor which indirectly influenced the debate on prisons and imprisonment in the closing years of the eighteenth century was the War of American Independence (1776-83). By 1776, about 1,000 prisoners were being transported annually to America. But with the outbreak of the American war, transportation to America was no longer possible. What, then, was to be done with the convicts? Parliament solved the problem with a 'temporary expedient': the prison hulks.

In 1776, an Act was passed which provided that any male 'lawfully convicted of great or petty larceny, or any other crime for which he shall be liable by law to a sentence of transportation . . . shall be punished by being kept to hard labour in the raising of sand, soil and gravel, and cleansing the river Thames, or any other service for the benefit of the navigation of the said river'. Responsibility for the convict labour force was vested in the justices of Middlesex. They, in turn, handed it over to one man, Duncan Campbell, whom they had appointed both overseer and contractor.

Campbell solved the problem of prison accommodation by acquiring two old ships, the *Justitia* and the *Censor*. The ships were dismantled, crudely fitted up

to house as many convicts as they would hold, and then moored in the Thames between Gallions Reach and Barking Reach. Thus it was that the first convict hulks came into service and a new misery was introduced.

By 1779, the hulks were becoming very overcrowded, but there was still no sign of an end to the American war. The government was compelled to take action. In 1779, the Blackstone and Eden Act extended the 'temporary' life of the hulks. To ease the overcrowding, certain local authorities were required to find room in their gaols for some of the convicts. But this was not a satisfactory long-term solution. The act therefore proposed the construction of one or more national penitentiaries.

Sir William Blackstone (1723-80), the jurist, and Sir William Eden (1744-1814), a radical politician, had been largely responsible for framing this legislation. They incorporated into the act a set of principles on which the proposed new penitentiaries should be run, and which might also offer guidance to local prison authorities faced with having to accommodate convicts until the new prison was built. Blackstone and Eden adopted Howard's recommendations, but added some of their own. For example, they suggested that the work given to the convicts should be 'of the hardest and most servile kind'. Prisoners should be adequately cared for, but were to have no luxuries or amusements of any kind. One welcome innovation was the recommendation that support and help in finding work should be given to ex-convicts after their discharge.

There was certainly no rush at local level to put Blackstone and Eden's recommendations into practice. The justices were for the most part a conservative body of men. It was only in a few counties that improvements went much beyond the provision of better sanitation. A requirement that Visiting Justices should be appointed to inspect the gaols was implemented in only about half a dozen counties.

Prison Reform in Gloucestershire

One county which did carry out substantial reforms was Gloucestershire, where the vast sum of nearly £50,000 was spent on rebuilding the county gaol and the local houses of correction. The prime instigator of this reform was Sir George Onesiphorous Paul, a county magistrate and one of Howard's disciples.

Before Paul's action, prisoners in Gloucester's county gaol were herded together in 'one dark pen'. He described how they were kept secure: 'A ponderous chain crossed this place of rest, and passing the middle link of each man's fetter, it is made fast at each end, and the whole number are threaded together ... There are present [1783] 40 prisoners so threaded together every night.' Of these, 14 were subsequently discharged as innocent. Sir George Paul estimated that for every one prisoner executed, three died of gaol-fever. Most of those who died were either debtors or prisoners awaiting trial.

After 1786, an entirely new regime was instituted. Prisoners were confined as far as possible in separate cells. All convicted prisoners were put to hard labour. Prisoners were visited every day by the prison governor and warders, and once or twice a week by the prison surgeon and chaplain. Visits from friends were strictly forbidden. All necessities were provided, but no alcohol or luxuries of any kind were allowed. All irons and chains, and all fees were abolished.

By making the justices, and not the prison governor, responsible for contracts for supplies, Sir George Paul reduced the possibility of fraud. He insisted on the need for accurate and detailed records. The governor, surgeon and chaplain were all required to keep a daily account of their activities. Visiting Justices had to put their own comments down in writing in a special 'Visitors' Book'. Finally, Paul drew up a list of regulations which spelled out, down to the last detail, the duties each official was required to perform. Gloucestershire's prison administration soon became a model for other enterprising counties to follow.

Government Action

In 1791, Parliament passed the first general Prisons Act. This stated that *all* prison establishments in England and Wales should be run according to the principles of Blackstone and Eden. Paul's influence showed in the more stringent responsibilities laid on the justices for the inspection, upkeep and management of the prisons. Although the Act was greeted with the usual apathy, its importance should not be overlooked, for it was the first time Parliament had expressly legislated for all prisons.

Transportation to Australia

The idea of transportation had never been completely abandoned, even though the United States was closed to British convicts after the Americans won their War of Independence, in 1783. Since 1776, several places, including West Africa and the Cape, had been suggested, but all had been reluctantly dropped as being unsuitable for one reason or another. However, after 1780, Captain Cook's voyages of discovery opened up a new possibility — Australia.

Not everyone was enthusiastic about renewing transportation. Some people believed that convicts could render useful service at home on public works projects. However, there were objections to this, as one Member of Parliament said in 1789: 'Landholders would not feel easy to have great numbers of convicts quartered in their neighbourhood. You will find nothing as good as transportation . . . Death, transportation and the Bridewell are . . . the only varieties of punishment that the manners of our country will admit of'. By 1791, the Prime Minister, William Pitt the Younger, was convinced that there was 'no cheaper mode of disposing of the convicts', and in any case, it was undoubtedly 'necessary . . . to send some of the most incorrigible criminals out of the kingdom'.

The first fleet of six convict ships and 759 convicts set sail in 1787. In 1790, further shiploads of convicts — 1,095 in all — were despatched; transportation to Australia was well and truly under way. After a terrible voyage lasting some six months, on meagre rations and in overcrowded, poorly ventilated conditions, the convicts finally reached Sydney. Some were employed directly by the military government of New South Wales. They worked in gangs under strict discipline, clearing the land, felling timber, building roads and houses or labouring in the dockyard. Others were assigned as labourers or domestic servants to government officials, to members of the New South Wales Corps, and, later on, to the free settlers who began to emigrate to the colony. Assignment was a chancy business, for everything depended on the kindness or otherwise of the master. Criticism of transportation was to grow in the nineteenth century, but for the time being, it seemed a cheap and satisfactory means of disposing of some of the king's less desirable subjects.

27 A notice on a bridge over a river in Dorset (1820's). A convenient way of dealing with trouble-makers was to give them a one-way ticket to Australia!

5
Attempts at Prison Reform

At the beginning of the nineteenth century, most of the prisons were still in the same sorry state in which John Howard had found them when he first began his tours of inspection in the 1770s. There was a marked lack of enthusiasm for reform among most members of Parliament. Opinion towards law-breakers had hardened since the French Revolution of 1789, and reactionary feelings were particularly noticeable in the House of Lords where several attempts to bring about minor reforms in the criminal law and in the prisons were blocked. The reformers' cause was hindered by the fact that many of them shared some of the liberal views which had inspired the French revolutionaries. As a result little progress towards reform was made in Parliament at that time. Activity outside Westminster, however, went on undiminished.

James Neild and J. T. Becher

The deplorable conditions in provincial gaols were revealed by the investigations of James Neild (1744-1814), a justice of the peace and subsequently High Sheriff of Buckinghamshire. Neild spent 12 years travelling around Britain, visiting well over 300 gaols, and a collected edition of his reports was published in 1812. His disclosures helped to bring about some small reforms concerning the maintenance of imprisoned debtors and also demonstrated the need for prison reform in general.

While Neild was making his country-wide survey, others concentrated their energies at more local level. In 1806, a newly-appointed Visiting Justice, the Rev. J.T. Becher, published a report denouncing the appalling state of the House of Correction at Southwell in Nottinghamshire and suggesting how it could be reformed. J.T. Becher managed to persuade the authorities to build a new bridewell, designed by him and administered along the lines he suggested. Briefly, Becher thought that the main purpose of imprisonment should be the reform of the prisoner, and that reform could best be promoted by providing work (on a profit-sharing basis), education and religious instruction. He believed that solitary confinement was the most effective way of disciplining prisoners who broke prison rules, but that it should be used only for that purpose.

The Society for the Improvement of Prison Discipline

Two years after Becher's report was published, a number of reformers formed a group known as the Society for the Improvement of Prison Discipline. Members of the Society carried out frequent gaol inspections and published reports of their findings as well as numerous pamphlets.

By 1816, the Society had attracted the support of some prominent Quaker families — the Gurneys, Hoares, Frys and Barclays. These people brought with them not only wealth and influence, but also a total commitment to social reform. The Society was able to make its views heard in Parliament since many of its members, among them Thomas Fowell Buxton and Samuel Hoare, were M.P.s.

The influence of the Society began to grow at a time when increasing crime and overcrowding in the gaols were beginning to cause public anxiety. Taking advantage of the situation, liberal-minded M.P.s began to step up the campaign for reform, and scored some minor successes. In 1815, all prison fees were abolished. In 1818, annual returns had to be made to the Home Secretary giving details of all persons committed to prison. These yearly statistics provided the reformers with valuable ammunition for their cause.

The Holford Committee, 1810

Several parliamentary committees of investigation were appointed during the period 1810-20, and they had great publicity value. One of the most important of them was the Select Parliamentary Committee on the Penitentiaries which was formed in 1810 under the chairmanship of G.P. Holford. By calling Sir George Paul and the Rev. J.T. Becher before the committee, Holford was able to publicize the reforms these two had carried out in Gloucester and Nottinghamshire respectively. Holford also summoned the keepers of Newgate and Horsemonger Lane gaols to give evidence, and, by doing so, was able to contrast the abuses prevalent in their gaols with the model establishments at Gloucester and Southwell.

The Holford committee was also very critical of transportation and the convict hulks, but realized that before they could be abolished a great deal of money would have to be spent on prison building. The committee urged that the plan for a new penitentiary, which had been shelved ever since it was first proposed in 1779, should therefore be implemented without delay. This produced some action, and by 1813, work had started on the model penitentiary at Millbank.

Elizabeth Fry (1780-1845)

It was at about this time that one of the most notable of prison reformers, Elizabeth Fry, first began her work in Newgate Gaol. Elizabeth Fry was born in 1780, the third daughter of Catherine and John Gurney, a successful Norwich merchant. Most of her childhood was spent in the happy atmosphere of the

28 Elizabeth Fry: Prison Reformer (1780-1845) (from an etching by Richard Dighton 1820).

family's comfortable home in Norfolk. Although John Gurney was a Quaker, he was not a very strict one and he allowed his daughter to lead the gay social life usual for any young girl in her well-off position.

When Elizabeth was 18, she had a religious experience which convinced her that the kind of life she was leading was too far removed from the old Quaker ideals. By 1799, she had adopted the close-fitting cap and black silk hood of the Quakeress. In the following year, she married Joseph Fry, a strict Quaker like herself, and a wealthy London merchant.

Elizabeth soon found her life of comfortable domesticity unsatisfying. Ever since her 'conversion', she had felt that God had singled her out for some

29 Elizabeth Fry reading to women prisoners at Newgate. Note the group of visitors on the left. Mrs Fry hoped that support for prison reform would grow if people were allowed to come and see what she and her helpers had achieved.

purpose, although she was not yet sure what it might be. In 1813, moved by a fellow Quaker's account of the sufferings of the prisoners, Elizabeth visited Newgate Gaol. By 1816, she knew that her vocation lay in prison work, and from then until her death in 1845, she was to devote all her energies to the campaign for prison reform.

One of Elizabeth Fry's first acts was to start a school for the children in the gaol. This was such a success that the women prisoners begged Elizabeth to find them something to do as well. In 1817, Elizabeth Fry, with the help of 11 Quakeresses and the wife of a clergyman, founded the Ladies' Association for the Improvement of the Female Prisoners in Newgate. This was the first of many ladies' committees which were soon set up in various parts of the country, and the forerunner of the prison visitors' associations which exist today.

The object of this first ladies' committee was 'to provide for the clothing, the instruction and the employment of the women; to introduce them to a knowledge of the Holy Scriptures, and to form in them, as much as possible, those habits of order, sobriety and industry, which may render them docile and peaceable whilst in prison, and respectable when they leave it'. Although the prison authorities were sceptical about its chances of success, they promised to help as much as possible.

The disused prison laundry was cleaned and whitewashed and turned into a workroom. The women worked in groups of about 12, under a monitor chosen by themselves. Within a year, Elizabeth was able to report that the prisoners 'knit from about 60 to 100 pairs of stockings and socks every month; they spin a little. The earnings of their work, we think, average about 18 pence [7½p] per week for each person'. Allowing the women to earn money was considered important. It gave them an incentive to work and offered tangible proof that what they were doing was useful.

More important from Elizabeth Fry's point of view was the need to transform the behaviour and if possible the character of the women through religious instruction. 'Our habit', she said, 'is constantly to read the scriptures to them twice a day; it has had an astonishing effect.' Visitors to the gaol were quick to notice how much the atmosphere in the women's wards had changed.

However, approval was by no means universal. Critics felt that even if it were possible to reform prisoners, the methods of Mrs Fry and her ladies' committee were not the ones most likely to achieve it. The lady visitors were accused of being naive, sentimental and exhibitionist. This last charge stemmed from the fact that Bible readings to the prisoners had become a public spectacle. Elizabeth Fry had been in favour of allowing members of the public to attend the readings so that they might see the kind of conditions in which she and her friends had to work, but she had never intended it to become a permanent practice. However naive and sentimental others might be, she herself had few illusions. She knew the process of reformation would be terribly slow and she was fully aware of the fact that prisoners would pretend to be repentant even when they clearly were not. Prison visitors, she said, should be 'as wise as serpents, and harmless as doves'.

Though she had begun her career in prison work as an amateur, Elizabeth Fry soon became an acknowledged expert. Her views on imprisonment, and on the treatment of female prisoners in particular, were too enlightened for the period in which she lived, and thus she did not live to see many of her principles adopted. Her idea of a separate prison for women, for instance, was not put into practice until after her death. But whenever prison reform was being discussed, her views were eagerly sought. In 1818, she was paid the signal honour of being invited to speak before a parliamentary committee on the prisons. From then until the early 1820s, her influence was probably at its peak. As the century wore on, however, there was less support for her views as opinion swung heavily in favour of a severer approach to prison discipline.

Sir Robert Peel (1788-1850)

While Elizabeth Fry had been busy at Newgate, the Society for the Improvement of Prison Discipline had kept up the pressure for government action. They collected statistics to back their case and to highlight the urgency of the need for reform. In 1820, they reported that 'of the 519 Gaols and Houses of

THE AWFUL FATE OF AN INCENDIARY.

This Engraving represents the Entrance of the County of Essex Convict Gaol—the Place of Execution on the Morning of the 27th of March, 1829, when James Cook, a boy only 16 years of age, suffered for the atrocious crime of setting on fire the premises of Mr. William Green, of Witham, farmer, with whom he lived as Cow Boy.

The Buildings and Stacks, which are represented as burning, furnish a true picture of the lamentable destruction of property occasioned by this wicked boy.

It is a melancholy fact, that there are offenders of the same cast still abroad, who by their conduct, show, that the disgraceful end of Cook has not operated as a sufficient example, to deter them from the commission of the like heinous crime; such, however, may be assured, that justice will ultimately overtake and punish them.

38

30 An extract from the Clelmsford Chronicle, 1829 (from *Law and Order in Essex*, Essex Record Office Publications, No. 54). Criminal law reform was a slow process — arson remained a capital offence until 1837.

31 A prisoner at work making shoes in his separate cell at Millbank (from *The Criminal Prisons of London*, by H. Mayhew and J. Binny, 1862).

32 'City of London System' (from J. Adshead's *Prisons and Prisoners*, 1845). The London prisons were notorious for their lack of order and discipline.

Correction in the United Kingdom, 23 only of these Prisons are divided for the classification of offenders; 59 have no division whatever to separate male from female prisoners: 136 have merely one division; and in 73 only has employment been introduced'.

In 1822, Sir Robert Peel replaced Lord Sidmouth as Home Secretary. More forward-looking and liberal than his predecessor, Peel was prepared to listen to the demands which assailed him from all sides for a reform in the criminal law and in the prison system.

Peel consolidated previous legislation and introduced some new reforms. Between 1825 and 1830, a series of statutes gradually reduced the number of offences punishable by death. For example, in 1832, housebreaking, horse- and sheep-stealing, and, in 1836, the coining of counterfeit money, all ceased to be capital offences.

By Peel's Prison Act of 1823, county justices were for the first time ordered to submit reports every three months to the Home Office 'upon every department of their prison administration'. They were required to accept John Howard's main principles: that the gaol-keeper should be a paid employee of the local authority; that prisons should be clean and secure; that all prisoners should undergo 'a reformatory regime' and that each prison should be thoroughly and regularly inspected. Gaolers were forbidden to extract fees of any kind whatsoever from their prisoners. Female prisoners were to be supervised by female warders, and the use of irons and chains and the imposition of all punishments notified to the justices.

Unfortunately, there was no system of national government inspection to ensure that this legislation would be obeyed. Furthermore, it only applied to

130 gaols: the county gaols, the prisons in 17 provincial towns and most of the London gaols. It did not cover London's three big debtor prisons nor the municipal gaols, which were reckoned at the time to be 'the filthiest and most abominable in the kingdom'.

The Millbank Penitentiary

The kind of prison regime which Peel had no doubt envisaged was already in operation in the new penitentiary at Millbank. Millbank's design represented a 'new look' in prison architecture. It was like a massive star with six three-storied pentagonal wings radiating out from a central building complex, in which the prison chapel was situated.

The prison was designed to take a maximum of 1,000 prisoners, each of whom was provided with a separate cell, fitted with lavatory, hand-basin, hammock and loom. From the outset, the staff included a medical officer, a chaplain, a master-manufacturer (to direct the prisoners' work), and a matron for the women prisoners. Prisoners had to undergo an initial period of solitary confinement, but during the rest of their time in prison they were allowed to associate with one another in groups. Although the building was not finished until 1821, prisoners were admitted as fast as each section was ready, and the first ones arrived in 1816.

Millbank was a forward-looking, enlightened experiment, but it was not without its teething troubles. In 1818, prisoners rioted in protest at the poor quality of the bread. Then outbreaks, in 1823, of scurvy, diarrhoea and dysentery, followed by a cholera epidemic, led to the temporary closure of the prison. A Parliamentary Committee appointed to enquire into the outbreak of sickness recommended various improvements such as better heating and ventilation and more education and daily exercise for prisoners. When the prison was reopened in 1824, greater care was taken to select the kind of prisoner who would be most likely to benefit from Millbank's reformatory regime: young persons, first offenders and those whose 'early habits and good character' gave hope of reform.

Millbank had been built at enormous cost, over £500,000. It was an ideal which county authorities could not hope to attain, bedevilled as they were by the need for economy. Added to this, they were genuinely perplexed by the vagueness of some of the requirements of Peel's Act — for example prisoners were to be classified, adequately fed and put to work, but no guidelines had been laid down to say exactly how this was to be done. This gave rise to endless controversy and permitted a wide variation in the treatment of prisoners.

The glaring abuses which many prison authorities allowed to go unchecked, and the ever-growing prison population (see Table 1) eventually forced the government to act.

Table 1

Number of persons charged with criminal offences and committed to prison for trial in England and Wales:

    For the seven years ending 31 December 1817   56,308
    For the seven years ending 31 December 1824   92,848
    For the seven years ending 31 December 1831 121,518

Note: Above figures exclude summary convictions, vagrants, debtors etc.
(*Source:* Select Committee on Secondary Punishments Report, 1832)

Prison Inspectors

In 1835 an act was passed 'for effecting greater uniformity of practice in the government of the several prisons in England and Wales, and for appointing inspectors of prisons in Great Britain'. The act provided for the appointment of five inspectors: one for Scotland, two covering the Home and Midland Counties, and two for the Northern and South Western Districts.

It soon became apparent just how revolutionary an act this was. Not only were the reports of the newly created inspectors of prisons to have an enormous influence on the shaping of national prison policy in the future, but the very fact that they had been appointed marked the beginning of the end of the 'do-it-yourself' policy which had been the hallmark of the prison system to date. The county justices continued to have overall responsibility for the running of the prisons and the gaols continued to be financed by local funds, but as each year went by the power of local authorities to act independently was increasingly restricted by the central government.

33 The tread-wheel. This hard labour machine, highly recommended by the Rev. Sydney Smith, was installed in many prisons after a suitable model was designed in 1818 by a Lowestoft engineer, William Cubitt.

The 1830s also saw a growing disenchantment with the humanitarian approach advocated by prison reformers since the beginning of the nineteenth century. Even in her most influential years, Elizabeth Fry had been criticized. Her most caustic critic, the Rev. Sydney Smith, wrote of her: 'Mrs. Fry is an amiable excellent woman... but hers is not the method to stop crimes. In prisons which are meant to keep the multitudes in order, and to be a terror to evildoers, there must be no sharing of profits – no visiting of friends – no education but religious education – no freedom of diet – no weavers' looms or carpenters' benches. There must be a great deal of solitude; coarse food, a dress of shame; hard, incessant, irksome, external labour; a planned and regulated and unrelenting exclusion of happiness and comfort.'

Many who had not shared Sydney Smith's views earlier began now to have second thoughts. The increase in crime and the continuing corruption in the country's gaols confirmed the hardliners in their view that humanitarian methods had failed. What was needed, they argued, was a tougher and more rigidly enforced system of prison discipline – a regime which would reform the criminal, certainly, but one which would also ensure that imprisonment was a proper deterrent and a punishment. It seemed to many people that the solution might be found in the United States, where experiments had been carried out into different methods of imprisonment. Some of these ideas were, in fact, to influence British prison policy for many years to come.

6
State Intervention

The Separate System

American experiments in the treatment of prisoners at the Eastern State Penitentiary, Philadelphia, and at Auburn Prison in New York State aroused considerable interest in Britain and in Western Europe. In 1832, William Crawford, an authority on prison discipline, was sent to America to study their methods at first hand.

The Eastern State Penitentiary, opened in 1829, was a brand new prison which pioneered the separate system: each prisoner was provided with his own separate cell in which he spent the whole of his imprisonment. There he ate, worked and slept in complete isolation. Even his daily hour of exercise was taken, alone, in a small yard adjoining his cell. His only human contact was with members of the prison staff.

Auburn Prison's silent system was a modified version of the separate system. The prisoners had separate cells, but were allowed to work together in gangs on public works projects. A rule of complete silence was imposed at all times, and obedience was enforced by means of the whip.

Crawford was particularly impressed by the Eastern State Penitentiary, and returned to England full of praise for the separate system. To his mind, it was better than the silent system both as a punishment and as a deterrent. As he said: "The whip inflicts immediate pain, but solitude inspires permanent terror.' His preference was significant, for in 1835, Crawford was appointed one of the prison inspectors for the Home and Midland Counties, and his views were listened to with respect.

34 A separate cell, equipped with hammock and loom, in Pentonville Prison (from *The Criminal Prisons of London*, 1862). Prisoners spent their time in isolation, apart from brief periods allotted to exercise and religious worship.

35 Reading Gaol (from *Prison Discipline* by the Rev. J. Field, 1846). The prisoners called it 'Read, Read, Reading Gaol' because the chaplain John Field, made them spend most of their time memorizing passages from the Bible. Oscar Wilde was imprisoned there (1895-97) and drew on this experience to write *De Profundis* and *Ballad of Reading Gaol*.

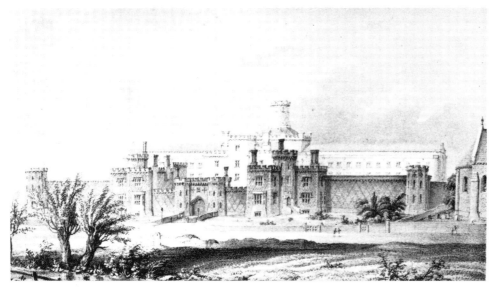

In 1838, the Third Report of the Inspectors of Prisons extolled the merits of separate confinement and recommended the construction of a new national penitentiary modelled on the Eastern State Penitentiary. The government accepted this advice. In 1839, the go-ahead was given to the building of the new prison and a circular was sent to all magistrates urging them to adopt the separate system.

In the meantime, some authorities had already introduced the silent system — since it was considerably cheaper to impose a rule of silence than to rebuild old prisons along cellular lines. After the government's new penitentiary, Pentonville, was opened in 1842, some local authorities followed suit. In 1845, for example, the new 'Prison Palace', Reading Gaol, was completed and the separate system introduced there.

Arguments about Transportation

In 1837, a Parliamentary Committee on Transportation was appointed under the chairmanship of Sir William Molesworth. The committee came down heavily against the practice of assigning convicts to work for private employers, describing it as little better than 'a lottery'. Convicts, it said, should not be sent to the settled areas, but should be restricted to the penal settlement on Norfolk Island off the coast of Australia, and to Van Dieman's Land (Tasmania).

Accepting the Molesworth Committee's advice, the government stopped transporting convicts to New South Wales in 1840 and, in the following year, put an end to assignment. A new scheme was drawn up whereby convicts transported for more than 15 years were to be sent to the rigorous and much feared penal settlement on Norfolk Island. Those sentenced to lesser terms were to be despatched to Van Dieman's Land, where they would be put to hard labour. After a time, and provided they had behaved well, the convicts were given a pass, or ticket of leave, which permitted them to work for a private employer for wages. But it was not long before Van Dieman's Land had become so overpopulated with convicts that disaster threatened. The arrival of growing numbers of free settlers in the territory and the near collapse of the colony's economy meant that, between 1844 and 1846, thousands of pass-holders were unable to find work.

In 1846, the government was forced to suspend transportation to Van Dieman's Land for two years, and to rethink its policy. Earl Grey, the Colonial Secretary, then produced a three-stage plan for dealing with those sentenced to transportation: the first stage of the sentence was to be spent in separate confinement in a cellular prison in Britain; the second stage consisted of hard labour either at home or in the colonies; for the third stage, the convict would be exiled indefinitely to one of the colonies on a ticket of leave. In order to carry out stages one and two, the government was forced to embark on building more prisons, for Millbank and Pentonville could not cope with the increased number of convicts to be accommodated.

Stage three of Grey's plan provoked a storm of protest, not only in Van Dieman's Land, where it had been hoped that the two-year suspension would become permanent, but also in Australia and elsewhere in the British Empire. No one wanted to receive Grey's 'exiles'. Annoyed by this show of unpatriotic fervour, the government was in no mood to give in, and, in any case, could not afford to do so. As a result transportation was resumed on the same lines as before.

36 Convicts going aboard a prison ship in Portsmouth Harbour, by E. Cooke, 1828. Conditions aboard the hulks were such that even the convicts' laundry hanging on the line was said to be crawling with vermin.

By the 1850s, however, the picture began to change. Although the great social reformer, Lord Shaftesbury, complained that the prospect 'of retaining our convicts in England is perfectly terrible', the trend of current opinion turned against transportation. *The Times*, which had originally welcomed Grey's policy, was deploring, in 1852, 'the infatuated perseverance in the present system', and claiming that transportation was a 'frightful inducement to the commission of crime'. It was also very much more expensive than keeping convicts in England. By 1851, all transportees were able to serve at least the first stage of their sentence in a British convict prison. It was clearly only a matter of time before the entire sentence could be served in this country.

In November, 1852, the last convict ship sailed for Hobart; in 1853, Van Dieman's Land ceased to be a penal settlement; by 1856, the Norfolk Island establishment was wound up. After the early 1850s, the only colony which actively welcomed convicts was Western Australia, and transportation there continued until 1867.

37 Scenes inside the prison hulk 'Defence' (from *The Criminal Prisons of London* by H. Mayhew and J. Binny, 1862).

The End of the Prison Hulks

In 1828, there were ten prison hulks housing 4,446 convicts, but their numbers declined steadily thereafter until by 1857 most had been abandoned. There were various reasons for this.

From the outset, the wretched conditions aboard these 'floating tombs' had resulted in a far higher death-rate than in ordinary gaols. In an attempt to suppress the abuses which a parliamentary investigation had disclosed, the government had in 1815 reorganized the management of the hulks, placing them under a newly-appointed superintendent, John Henry Capper.

During the early part of his long 'reign', which lasted from 1815 to 1847, Capper introduced a number of improvements. Convicts were segregated in cells in groups of 10 or 12. Their diet was improved, and greater supervision helped to eliminate much of the vice and corruption which had flourished in the past. Medical officers were appointed and each hulk had its own chaplain. A systematic attempt was made to provide regular work. For the adults, this meant hard labour in the neighbouring dockyards, but they were at least allowed to keep part of their earnings, some of which was set aside to be paid out in a lump sum on their discharge. Juvenile offenders were segregated aboard the hulk *Euryalus* where they were taught a trade which might be useful to them on release.

In his later years, however, Capper left more of the work to his clerk. By 1847, reports of maladministration had become so frequent — even the *Euryalus* was described as a 'school for vice' — that Parliament was forced to investigate. The net result was that Capper, by then in his 70s, 'resigned', and the whole administration was once again overhauled. But the days of the hulks were clearly numbered.

By 1857, only the *Defence* remained. On 14 July 1857, this, the last of the hulks, went up in smoke. Fire brigades rushed to the scene from Woolwich Arsenal and Dockyard nearby, but the fire had spread to the hulk's coal store, and nothing could save it. For those who had endured a spell on board the hulks, the news of the demise of the *Defence* must have seemed a fitting end to a system which had brought so much misery.

One of the chief reasons for transportation, and the sole justification for the hulks, had been the lack of suitable prisons on land in which to house convicts. As a result, the problems in Van Dieman's Land in 1846, which forced the government to build more prisons, also indirectly helped to bring an end to the prison hulks.

New Prisons

After 1846, the government embarked on a spate of prison building. A prison in which convicts could serve the second, hard-labour stage of their sentence was built at Portland in Dorset, where the great mole of Portland harbour remains a monument to the hundreds of convicts who laboured to build it. Prisons conveniently situated for dockyard work were established at Portsmouth and Chatham. Dartmoor, originally built for prisoners of war in 1806, was transformed into a new model gaol in 1850.

In 1850, the government also appointed a new body, the Directors of Convict Prisons, to bring under direct government control all establishments dealing with prisoners sentenced to transportation. The chairman of the Directors was Colonel (later Sir) Joshua Jebb. Jebb's growing dislike both of transportation and of the hulks led to legislation which hastened their abolition. By the Penal Servitude Acts of 1853 and 1857, instead of transportation, prisoners could be sentenced to a term of penal servitude in a British gaol. This still followed Grey's three-stage plan, the only difference being that the whole of the sentence was served in Britain. These convict prisons followed the same regime as the government's new model prison, Pentonville, opened in 1842.

The nineteenth-century writer on prisons, Hepworth Dixon, has left us this description of Pentonville in the 1850s:

> The prison consists of five wings or galleries, radiating from a point, the view from which is very striking, and at the same time very unprisonlike. On the sides of four of these galleries the cells are situate and numbered . . . Now

38 A model of Pentonville Prison (from *Prisons and Prisoners,* by J. Adshead, 1845). Prisoners were exercised in groups in the long enclosures on each side of the entrance hall. The circular areas were divided into tiny yards where dangerous prisoners or invalids took solitary exercise supervised by the warder stationed at the centre.

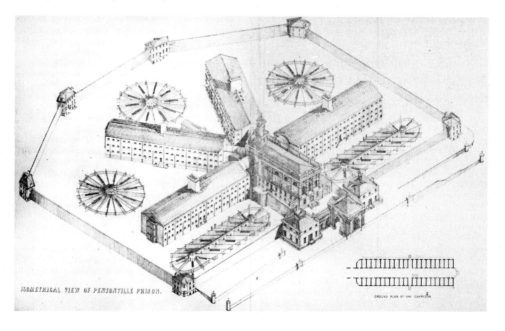

ISOMETRICAL VIEW OF PENTONVILLE PRISON.

GROUND PLAN OF ONE CORRIDOR

39 Extraordinary measures were taken to separate the convicts even during group exercise. Prisoners were positioned at intervals of approximately five metres, their places marked by knots made in a rope. They had to hold the rope and march briskly round in circles (from *The Criminal Prisons of London* by H. Mayhew and J. Binny, 1862).

let us enter a cell . . . Its arrangement and fittings seem to be faultless. It is sufficiently large . . . It is admirably ventilated . . . and by means of warm air is kept at an even and agreeable temperature. It has even the luxuries of a water-closet, and of an unlimited supply of warm and cold water. The bedding is clean and good; the food is also good, and plentiful in supply . . . Yet although there are so many expensive luxuries about him . . . no prisoner, except in rare cases, likes it. Many fear it [solitary confinement] worse than they do death.

As Hepworth Dixon points out, the separate system had eliminated the old abuses, but in so doing had introduced new terrors — of silence and solitude.

Prisoners in general stayed in Pentonville for between 15 months and two years. The daily routine never varied. At 6 a.m. the cells were unlocked and scrubbed out. Work, usually weaving or mat-making, commenced at 6.30 a.m. During working hours the cell doors were left open, but the prisoners were under constant surveillance. There were short breaks for meals, and for writing letters, which were censored. Half-an-hour's exercise, in silence in the prison quadrangle, was allowed, as well as attendance at a 30-minute service in the prison chapel. At 7 p.m. work stopped. From then until lights out at 9 p.m., the prisoners were allowed to read books of an 'improving' nature. No work was done on Sundays, but long religious services occupied most of the morning and afternoon. Relatives and friends could visit the prisoners for 15 minutes every three months, but this was later reduced to 20 minutes every six months.

Prisoners in Pentonville were virtually stripped of their identities. Each prisoner was known only by his cell number, inscribed on a brass badge affixed to his prison uniform. Whenever he left his cell, he had to wear a distinctive brown cloth cap, with a mask attached to conceal his face. One visitor commented that this made the prisoners seem more like ghosts than men: 'For the eyes glistening through the apertures in the mask give the notion of a spirit peeping out from behind it, so that there is something positively terrible in the idea that there are men whose crimes have caused their features to be hidden from the world.'

During the six years following the completion of Pentonville, 54 new prisons were built in Britain on the same lines, although there were some variations in the prison regime.

Some London Prisons

Brixton In 1853, Brixton, a former Surrey House of Correction, was taken over as a national convict prison for women.

Prisoners spent their first four months in separate confinement, after which they were allowed to work together — at needlework, laundering, etc. A rule of silence was imposed during working hours, but prisoners could talk at specified times of the day.

Some women found the monotony of their existence so unbearable that they would wound themselves, sometimes to the point of death, in order to be transferred to the prison infirmary for 'a change'. Brixton had a special maternity ward, to which women from Millbank could also be sent. Children up to the age of two were allowed to remain with their mothers, and by 1860 the rule had been altered to allow mothers to keep their children with them right up until their discharge.

Some prisons in London were reserved for those serving sentences of up to two years. Among these were Cold Bath Fields, Wandsworth and Holloway.

Cold Bath Fields The silent system had been introduced here in 1834. By 1854, Cold Bath Fields was an all-male establishment, containing 1,495 prisoners.

Prisoners laboured either at the treadwheel or at oakum-picking. Oakum-picking consisted of unravelling lengths of tarry old rope. The fibres or oakum thus produced were used for caulking wooden ships. As these became obsolete, the usefulness of oakum-picking diminished. In its heyday about 500 prisoners could be seen picking oakum in a vast room at Cold Bath Fields, in complete silence.

Wandsworth This prison, opened in 1851, took both men and women prisoners. There was no treadwheel, because it was considered too expensive to

40 The prison chapel, Pentonville (from *The Criminal Prisons of London* by H. Mayhew and J. Binny, 1862).

41 Prisoners and their babies in the nursery of the women's convict prison, Brixton (from *The Criminal Prisons of London* by H. Mayhew and J. Binny, 1862).

42 Oakum picking under the silent system at Cold Bath Fields House of Correction (from *The Criminal Prisons of London*, by H. Mayhew and J. Binny, 1862). Prisoners had to shred lengths of old tarry rope into fibre or oakum, which was used for caulking wooden ships.

install. Instead, those sentenced to hard labour were put to work in the pump-house, pumping water up into the cisterns on the roof. To achieve this, each prisoner had to turn the pump-handles nearly 5,000 times per day. Other hard-labour prisoners spent their time alone in their cells working on the crank. This pointless machine was invented by a Mr Gibbs of Pentonville in 1846. It consisted of 'a narrow iron drum placed on legs, with a long handle on one side which, when turned, causes a series of cups or scoops in the interior to revolve'. As the drum went round, the cups scooped up and emptied sand which had been placed in the lower part of the interior, rather like a dredging-machine. It was extremely hard work and yet achieved nothing.

Prisoners not sentenced to hard labour were employed making shoes or mats. Women were given needlework, cleaning and laundering to do.

Holloway Holloway's foundation stone bore the inscription: 'May God preserve the City of London, and make this place a terror to evil-doers.' The prison was built on the Pentonville pattern, with 438 separate cells, and was completed in 1852. It was intended to replace Newgate, but because of the shortage of prison accommodation, Newgate continued to be used, chiefly for housing prisoners awaiting trial at the Old Bailey.

Horsemonger Lane was Surrey's main county prison. It did not operate a system of separate confinement, and indeed had very little system at all. 'The visitor is painfully impressed with the absence of all rule,' wrote Hepworth Dixon. Prisoners 'saunter about their dungeon, or loll upon the floor, listening to the highly spiced stories of their companions, well content to be fed at the expense of the county.' Picking oakum was the only work available on the men's side of the prison, but 'by 12 or one o'clock many have finished, and the rest of the day is given up to laziness'.

Such striking differences in the treatment of prisoners demonstrated the need for greater government control over the prisons. This was further emphasized in the mid-nineteenth century by revelations of cruelty and the savage treatment of prisoners at Birmingham and Leicester.

Prison Scandals

By 1853, rumours began to circulate of terrible cruelties at Birmingham gaol. A Royal Commission found that prisoners were being set impossible tasks on the crank, and that if they failed to complete their work, they received no food.

43 Debtor prisoners whiling away their time in the Queen's Bench Prison (from *Twice Round the Clock* by G. A. Sala, 1862). The debtors were allowed to preserve a shred of dignity — their letters came addressed, not to the prison, but to No. 1 Belvedere Place!

Prisoners who became hysterical were punished by being placed in a strait-jacket. Others were repeatedly whipped. Medical care was so poor that prisoners sometimes died in their cells out of sheer neglect. Conditions at Leicester Gaol caused equal disquiet, and were also investigated by a Royal Commission. As a result criminal proceedings were taken against the governors and medical officers of both gaols. The affair was widely publicized and shook public confidence in the ability of local authorities to run their own gaols.

If the scandals at Birmingham and Leicester pointed to the need for more central government control, a crime wave in the 1860s gave rise to a demand for a more deterrent and punitive policy. In London, in particular, there had been a spate of robberies with violence in which the attackers had tried to garrotte or strangle their victims.

A House of Lords Select Committee on Prisons and Prison Discipline, led by the Earl of Carnarvon, stressed the need for deterrence. Moral reformation 'forms part of a sound penal system', said the Committee, but 'in the interests of society and the criminal himself . . . the reformation of offenders should always be accompanied by due and effective punishment'.

Government Legislation

With pressure coming from both sides, the government was forced into action. By the Prisons Act of 1865, local authorities were ordered to erect separate cells for all prisoners. There was to be no distinction between houses of correct-tion and prisons. All prison labour was to be standardized into two classes. First-class labour meant the treadwheel, the crank and stone-breaking. Second-class labour was not as closely defined, but was to be any kind of hard physical exertion the Home Secretary might specify. Prisoners' diets had to conform with Home Office regulations.

The Act was unrelentingly severe when it came to punishments. Prison governors had the authority to punish any prisoner by inflicting solitary confinement for three days and nights on bread and water. Visiting Justices could inflict a whole month in a punishment cell, or a flogging. The use of chains, irons and other methods of restraint were specifically authorized. A code of rules, minutely detailed, was to be observed in all prisons.

Each prison had to have a doctor and an Anglican chaplain, and a coroner's inquest was to be held on every prisoner who died in gaol. One other welcome innovation was the authorization of some form of grant-in-aid out of public funds to assist prisoners on their discharge.

The act led to the closure of several town gaols, for the smaller boroughs could not afford to rebuild their gaols along the new lines specified. The number of prisons in England and Wales dwindled to 113.

Uniformity in prisons was further assisted by the act of 1869, which abolished sentences of imprisonment for debt. Debtors had always been a problem since they could not by law be prevented from bringing into prison food, tobacco

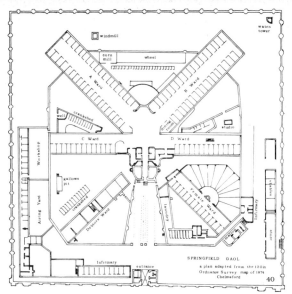

44 Plan of Springfield Gaol, Essex, 1874 (from *Law and Order in Essex*, Essex Record Office Publications, No. 54). Note the cranksheds, the row of tread-wheels and the separate women's ward, with its adjoining exercise yards.

and other luxuries denied to criminal prisoners. Their freedom to receive visitors and to make contact with the outside world was also incompatible with strict prison discipline.

The employment of prisoners was another controversial topic. The act of 1865 had not ruled out productive employment. In some prisons, profits from prison industries were considerable. Wakefield Gaol's mat-making industry, for example, grossed annual profits of £40,000 in the 1870s. Some of this was used to offset gaol expenses. Although the Treasury made annual grants towards the upkeep of local prisons, it was the county ratepayers who paid the lion's share. The counties therefore had an interest in allowing profit-making prison industries to continue. The Home Office, on the other hand, did not want the prisons to be run like factories. Clearly, there was a conflict of interests.

Nationalizing the Prisons

By the 1870s, there was much resentment, particularly among ratepayers in rural districts, at the high level of the rates. In 1874, a new government came into power which promised to do something to reduce them.

The government soon realized that if the counties were relieved of the responsibility of financing the local gaols, this would at one stroke ease the ratepayers' burden and at the same time make it possible to bring the gaols under one central authority, thus ending the tiresome arguments about such matters as prison industries.

There were protests that such a policy represented an unwarrantable extension of government authority. In the end, however, the prospect of shedding the hefty financial burden of bringing the gaols up to the standards required by the 1865 act, and maintaining them year by year, was too attractive to be resisted.

In 1877, a Prisons Act was passed which at last brought all the prisons in England and Wales firmly under central government control and marked the beginning of a new chapter in prison history.

7

The Growth of a Social Conscience

The Du Cane Regime

After the Prisons Act of 1877, local prisons were administered by a Board of Prison Commissioners, while the convict prisons continued to be run by the Directors of Convict Prisons.. However, since both of these bodies shared the same chairman, Lieutenant-Colonel (later Sir) Edmund Du Cane (1830-1903), a coordinated policy for all prisons was made possible.

On 1 April 1878, when the Prison Commission was officially launched, the prison population numbered just over 31,000, of which roughly two-thirds were accommodated in local prisons. Du Cane immediately closed 38 of these. Others were gradually phased out, so that by 1894, there were only 56 local prisons left.

Du Cane tackled the enormously difficult task of reorganization with economy, speed and efficiency. One of his main achievements was the establishment of a prison staff structure based on military lines. Before 1877, favouritism and patronage in the appointment of staff were commonplace. Du Cane made it clear that henceforth appointments were to be made solely on merit.

Prisoners had often been placed in authority over their fellow-inmates. At Cold Bath Fields, for example, Du Cane found that no fewer than 82 prisoners were employed as guards. This practice was also stopped.

The new prison staff was organized on a pyramidal basis. At the top was the governor, followed by the chief warder, principal warders, warders and assistant warders. Precise rules of conduct were laid down for each rank. Warders who broke regulations could be dismissed, and staff were warned that 'any instances of improper behaviour or ill-treatment of a prisoner' would be most severely dealt with.

As far as the prisoners were concerned, under Du Cane discipline and uniformity were the order of the day. Little allowance was made for differences in age and state of health of prisoners. All were subjected to the same rigorous regime, called the Progressive Stage System, which was based on the idea of separate confinement and silence. Its slogan was 'hard bed, hard fare, hard labour'.

The system consisted of four stages, and as the prisoner progressed through

45 The numbing monotony of prison regime in the late nineteenth century is conveyed in this picture by Gustave Doré of the exercise yard at Newgate, 1872.

them his conditions gradually improved. A marks system was introduced, and each prisoner had to earn 224 marks to complete a stage. Marks were awarded for good behaviour and hard work, but they could also be deducted for misconduct and idleness. No prisoner could move on to the next stage before earning his full quota of marks.

46 A convict in chains on public works at Portsmouth, 1879. Note the broad arrowed clothing, which was to remain the mark of the convict until the 1920's.

47 Convict caricatures — prisoners being photographed for the 'Rogues' Gallery', 1889.

The first stage, unrelieved separate confinement, lasted for between one and six months. Prisoners were not allowed to keep family mementos, and news of the outside world was excluded. Even the pleasure of looking at the sky was denied, cell-windows being fitted with opaque glass. Prisoners sentenced to hard labour (first-class) had to spend at least six hours a day on strenuous, unproductive labour — usually working the crank. Male prisoners were not allowed a mattress on their plank bed. School instruction and books were forbidden.

Exercise in the open was not permitted until stage two, and then only on Sundays in the bleak prison yard. At this stage, industrial work and some education were allowed. Stage three was much the same, except that by then the prisoner could have a mattress for six days a week. Not until stage four was the prisoner allowed to receive visits, write letters or read library books.

The 'progressiveness' of the system was only apparent to long-sentence prisoners, but they only formed two per cent of the total prison population. The rest were serving sentences of between one week and six months. As a result, few prisoners were able to pass beyond stage one, let alone experience the relative advantages of stage four.

The effect of the Progressive Stage System was devastating, and has been
blamed for turning the convict into an object of contempt. 'Men and women
went into prisons as people. They came out mentally numbed and some of them
insane; they became the creatures, ugly and brutish in appearance, stupid and
resentful in behaviour, unemployable and emotionally unstable, which the
Victorian middle classes came to visualize whenever they thought of prisoners.'

The Gladstone Committee

In 1894, as criticism was mounting, the government appointed a special committee of inquiry under Herbert Gladstone, Under-Secretary of State at the Home
Office. The feeling of the Gladstone Committee is summed up in the following
extract from their report: 'The great, and as we consider the proved danger of
this highly centralized system has been and is that while much attention has
been given to organization, finance, order, health of prisoners and prison statistics, the prisoners have been treated too much as a hopeless or worthless

48 Boys exercising at Tothill Fields Prison (from *The Criminal Prisons of London* by
H. Mayhew and J. Binny, 1862). There was little special treatment for juvenile prisoners
until the twentieth century

49 High Beech Probation Home, Redhill, Surrey, founded in 1950 by the London Police Court Mission (now the Rainer Foundation), one of the voluntary bodies which provided the probation service until the State took over in 1940.

element of the community, and the moral as well as the legal responsibilities of the Prison Authorities has been held to cease when they pass outside the prison gates.'

With the retirement of Sir Edmund Du Cane in 1894, responsibility for implementing the Gladstone Committee's recommendations fell to his successor, Evelyn Ruggles-Brise (1857-1935).

Juvenile Offenders

The Gladstone Committee drew attention to the lack of any special treatment for juvenile offenders. It is true that, by the late nineteenth century, an alternative to imprisonment had been provided for children under the age of 16. Instead of being committed to prison, they might be sent to a reformatory, where they were housed and fed and subjected to a disciplinary regime which included basic education and instruction in a trade. For young offenders over the age of 16, however, there was no alternative to prison. The Gladstone Committee had suggested that the government should experiment with establishing a penal reformatory along the lines of the Elmira Reformatory in New York State.

In 1897, Ruggles-Brise visited the American reformatory. He described Elmira as a 'bold experiment', but thought its maximum age limit of 30 years too high, and its cultural and recreational facilities too lavish. In 1900 *The Times* sounded a cautionary note. If the British were accused of being too preoccupied with deterring the offender, said *The Times*, in America, there was 'too much a tendency to think of the criminal as an interesting object to be reformed'.

It was in such a climate of opinion that the experiment began with eight young prisoners in a separate wing at Bedford Gaol. Results were so encouraging that it was decided to devote part of the convict prison at Borstal in Kent for the reformatory training of young prisoners up to the age of 21. This is how the borstals got their name.

The Borstal experiment was very much part of the penal system, and was carried out in closed-prison conditions. Boys serving sentences of a minimum of six months were selected from the London prisons and taken to Borstal. The first batch arrived in chains! In 1903, the scheme was extended to Dartmoor.

The fundamental principles of the new treatment were: '(1) strict classification; (2) firm and exact discipline; (3) hard work; (4) organized supervision on discharge'. The regime included physical drill, trade instruction and basic education. After-care was provided by the Borstal Association, a largely voluntary organization. After-care — the work of resettling the boys in the community — was not just an 'extra', but was regarded as an integral part of borstal training.

In 1908, the borstal experiment received legal sanction through the Prevention of Crime Act. Courts of Assize and Quarter Sessions could now sentence 16- to 21-year-olds 'to detention under penal discipline in a Borstal Institution for a term of not less than one year nor more than three years' instead of imprisonment. In general the borstal sentence was longer than the equivalent prison sentence — the Prison Commissioners were convinced that six months was too short a period for the borstal training to have the desired effect.

The Children Act of 1908 reinforced the idea that young offenders were to be treated differently from adults. The act spelled out the principle that no child should be sentenced to imprisonment unless he were judged so unruly that no other course was possible. Special Juvenile Courts were established, quite separate from the ordinary courts, and the general public was excluded from them. Juvenile offenders who were refused bail were held until their trial in one of the Remand Homes provided for by the act.

Other Special Cases

Persistent offenders The Prevention of Crime Act of 1908 provided that offenders with a record of three or more previous convictions could be sentenced to a maximum of 10 years' Preventive Detention in addition to the normal sentence. This measure was intended to protect the public from dangerous criminals, but the courts, perhaps not wishing to impose what was in effect a 'double' sentence, made little use of the provision.

Mentally deficient offenders An act of 1913 provided that mentally deficient offenders should be committed to special mental asylums. Since the 1860s, prisoners certified as insane had been removed from prison and placed in the newly-built mental asylum for criminals, Broadmoor. But there had been no special provision for prisoners suffering from less severe mental disorders, and the 1913 act was therefore welcome.

Probation The Probation of Offenders Act, 1908 empowered the courts to appoint their own probation officers to supervise those offenders who had been released on probation instead of being imprisoned. Supervision had previously been carried out by voluntary organizations, notably the Church of England Temperance Society. Voluntary workers still had a role to play, but the act laid the foundations of a professional probation service.

Prison Conditions

There were some minor improvements in prison conditions in the early years of the twentieth century. The prison diet was made more generous and more exercise was permitted. Facilities for education were also a little better. On the whole, however, the regime remained very strict. For example, the time allowed for instruction, and the provision of books, were inadequate. Similarly, although the crank and the tread wheel were abolished, oakum-picking, so characteristic of nineteenth-century prison labour, continued. In 1910-11, over 20 per cent of prisoners were employed in this or similar unproductive work.

Prisoners were classified into three Divisions. Division 1 was intended for those who had committed offences of 'conscience', such as suffragettes and conscientious objectors. They were allowed a number of privileges with regard to food, clothing and work. Minor offenders were classified in Division 2. However, unless the courts specifically ordered otherwise, the majority of prisoners were automatically relegated to Division 3, with or without hard labour.

Suffragettes and Conscientious Objectors

The campaign to secure the vote for women brought large numbers of female prisoners, most of whom were classified in Divisions 1 or 2. The Vote for Women campaign presented the authorities with an awkward problem. The suffragettes were no ordinary criminals. Furthermore many of them were highly connected and, as such, received preferential treatment, often against their will.

Lady Constance Lytton, for example, demonstrated how little sympathy ordinary women prisoners were shown by disguising herself as plain 'Miss Jane Wharton'. She was sentenced to a fortnight's imprisonment, in Division 3, with hard labour. There was a good deal of embarrassment when 'Miss Wharton's' true identity was revealed. Lady Constance Lytton's experiences, described in her book *Prisons and Prisoners* (1914), and those of other imprisoned suffragettes helped to inform the public about prison conditions.

The First World War (1914-18) produced another kind of non-criminal offender — the conscientious objector. Conscientious objectors refused to take part in the war because they did not believe it was right to kill, and many were imprisoned for their beliefs. Among them Stephen Hobhouse and A. Fenner Brockway were particularly important. After the war, they produced a book, *English Prisons Today* (1922) which was severely critical of the prison system.

50 The forced feeding of suffragettes on hunger strike while in prison became a political issue in the campaign to secure the vote for women.

The Paterson Era

In 1921, Sir Evelyn Ruggles-Brise retired, and Maurice Waller became the new Chairman of the Prison Commission. More significant, however, was the appointment in 1922 of Alexander Paterson as Prison Commissioner in charge of borstal institutions. Then aged 38, Paterson was younger than any governor in the prison service.

Even before the war, Paterson's views had carried weight. As early as 1908, he had been consulted about the drafting of the Children Act. Although his main concern both then and later was the treatment of young offenders, his interest ranged over the whole field of penal reform. His international reputation was firmly established between the two World Wars, when he and Sir Maurice Waller drew up the 'Minimum Rules for the Treatment of Prisoners' which was adopted by the League of Nations.

Paterson never became Chairman of the Prison Commission. He saw himself as 'a missionary not an administrator', and refused appointment to the post. In fact, he had no need of promotion, for his personal influence was sufficient without it. He was not only a reformer of vision and energy, but possessed enough personality and charm to inspire others with his own enthusiasm.

The liberalizing influence of the new regime was soon felt in the prisons. Prisoners were permitted to talk during working hours. Visiting arrangements were improved. The time allowed for each visit could be converted into fewer, but longer, visits. In addition, outsiders interested in prisoners' welfare were allowed into the prisons. Male visitors were allowed into the men's prisons. Lady visitors had been permitted to visit the women's prisons since the foundation, in 1900, of the Lady Visitors' Association. Being neither prisoners' relatives nor part of the prison staff, they played an important intermediate role, talking over prisoners' problems with them and helping in numerous ways.

The early 1920s saw the removal of rules which prisoners had found unnecessarily degrading. The 'convict hair-crop' was abolished. The broad arrows on prison clothing which had been the trademark of the convict were removed. Other improvements were the introduction of a prison newspaper and the relaxation of the rules on allowing prisoners to keep pictures and photographs. The old Victorian regime was at last on the way out. In this respect, perhaps nothing was more significant than the abolition, in 1930, of the period of separate confinement which the prisoners had previously had to undergo at the start of their sentence.

Change was, however, most marked in the treatment of juvenile offenders. Here Paterson's views on juvenile crime are important, since they determined the kind of treatment he recommended. Paterson was convinced of the connexion between deprivation and crime. He believed that bad housing, lack of education and unemployment produced an environment favourable to crime, and that it was the inability to say 'no' to temptation which was the fundamental cause of juvenile crime. In his view every sane person was responsible for his actions and had the freedom to choose between right and wrong. There was good, he said, in 'every British lad'. With the right kind of education and training, a boy could acquire enough willpower and self-discipline to enable him to choose what was right and reject what was wrong.

Believing in the character-building qualities of a public-school education, Paterson set out to reform the borstals on those lines. Each borstal was organized into 'houses'. To create an atmosphere of school rather than prison, the staff wore ordinary civilian clothes. Outdoor activities were encouraged and inter-house games became part of the character-building process. Education, formerly confined to the 'three R's', was widened. Religion remained the 'first line of defence against crime', but the need for social responsibility was stressed. The selection of staff totally dedicated to these ideals was fundamental to the success of the scheme. 'The Borstal system has no merit apart from the Borstal staff,' Paterson wrote. 'It is men and not buildings who will change the hearts and minds of misguided lads.'

Until 1930, all borstals were closed institutions. It was difficult to eradicate the prison-like atmosphere which pervaded buildings which had been built as penal institutions. Even after an old industrial school at Feltham in Middlesex had been converted into a borstal, it still had the feel of Wormwood Scrubs about it. As Paterson said: 'You cannot train men for freedom in conditions of captivity.' The logical, but revolutionary, next step was an open institution.

An Open Borstal

The first open borstal was Lowdham Grange near Nottingham, and its first 'guinea-pigs' were boys selected from Feltham. They actually marched the whole way — over 200 kilometres — to Lowdham Grange.

> There were no guards, no uniforms, nothing to distinguish the company from any boys' club on the hike . . . One of the staff who was on that journey once characterized it as an act of faith, which indeed it was. There was no previous experience by which it was possible to judge the chances of success or the chances that the boys might break away or misbehave. But it passed without incident. The boys at first lived in tents or huts while they levelled the ground and built their own institution, which is now a harmonious and dignified group of buildings in the midst of its own gardens and farm lands, with no high wall or barbed wire to cut it off from the surrounding countryside. And so we got our first open Borstal. (Quoted from *Borstal, a Critical Survey*, by W. A. Elkin and D. B. Kittermaster, 1952)

By 1939, there were four open and five closed borstals. Yet in 1938 for example, only 17 per cent of the total borstal population (2,020) were in open institutions. A study carried out by the Borstal Association in 1939 showed that 77 per cent of boys from Lowdham Grange had not been reconvicted, compared with 50 per cent of boys from the closed borstal at Portland. These results were not particularly surprising, since it was only the most promising boys who were selected for training in open borstals. Furthermore, at that time, being sent to an open borstal was a coveted privilege, and most boys responded to the trust placed in them.

An Open Prison

Experimentation with an open prison for adults began in 1936, at New Hall Camp near Wakefield. In May of that year, 20 prisoners, two prison officers and a house master spent a week there, and, from January 1937, moved in on a permanent basis.

It is difficult to recreate now the mood of buoyant optimism and confidence which predominated in the late 1930s. The reformed borstal training seemed to be working well, and although there had been considerable local opposition to them the open institutions promised to be even more successful. Plans were afoot to close Pentonville and to replace Holloway and Aylesbury prisons with two open institutions to be built on a site already acquired at Stanwell in Middlesex. In the event, the outbreak of the Second World War in 1939 caused these plans to be shelved.

No substantial changes could be contemplated during the war, and it was not until after peace returned in 1945 that Parliament could begin to consider penal policy once again. But then, in 1947, Alexander Paterson died, thus bringing to a close an era of prison history in which he had played a leading role.

51 Wetherby Open Borstal, near Leeds. This young man hands in his pass at the gates on his way to work for a private employer while serving a borstal sentence.

8
Prisons Today and Tomorrow

Since the Second World War, English penal policy has been guided by two main principles: that as far as possible people should be kept out of prison; and that if offenders have to be imprisoned, then every effort should be made to rehabilitate them.

The Criminal Justice Act, 1948
The first major piece of post-war legislation was the Criminal Justice Act of 1948. Its aim is summed up in Rule 6 of the act: 'The purpose of training and treatment of convicted prisoners shall be to establish in them the will to lead a good and useful life on discharge, and to fit them to do so'.

The act eliminated the last vestiges of the Victorian regime by abolishing penal servitude and hard labour — both of which had ceased to have any real meaning. The classification of prisoners into Divisions had proved unsuccessful, and was dropped.

The rest of the act's provisions fall into two broad categories — those of a reformative nature and those which were purely deterrent. The former included the introduction of corrective training, alternatives to imprisonment and changes in the probation arrangements. The latter included preventive detention as a sentence in its own right and the creation of 'starkly punitive' detention centres which were intended to administer a 'short, sharp shock' to young delinquents.

The 1948 act may not have reduced the prison population (see Table II) but it has to some extent changed its composition.

Table II
Average Daily Number of People in Prisons, Borstals
and Detention Centres in England and Wales

1938	11,086
1948	19,765
1958	25,379
1968	32,461

(*Source: People in Prison, England and Wales*, Home Office, 1968)

After 1948, two trends can be noted. Firstly, there was a drop in the number of short-sentence prisoners. As the act intended, the courts preferred a probation order or conditional discharge to a prison sentence of two to five weeks. Secondly, the number of long-sentence prisoners rose. As Table III below shows, the proportion of long-sentence prisoners in relation to the rest of the prison population has greatly increased since before the war. This has produced considerable security problems.

Table III
Length of Prison Sentence Imposed (Males and Females)*

	1938	1948	1958	1968
Up to 2 weeks	8,820	3,366	3,030	2,932
Over 2 weeks up to 5 weeks	7,475	5,595	4,922	3,765
Over 5 weeks up to 3 months	7,043	8,925	8,398	6,930
Over 3 months up to 6 months	3,947	6,447	6,710	7,801
Over 6 months up to 12 months	1,881	4,775	4,843	5,858
Over 12 months up to 18 months	694	2,361	2,085	3,179
Over 18 months up to 3 years	581	2,478	2,906	4,059
Over 3 years up to 5 years	158	617	733	1,086
Over 5 years	47	123	348	364
Life	14	30	40	95

*Including periods imposed in cases of fine default but excluding sentences of corrective training and preventive detention.
(*Source: People in Prison, England and Wales*, Home Office, 1968)

52 Winston Green Prison, Birmingham, from which the train robber, Charles Wilson, escaped in 1964.

Security in prisons had also been made more difficult by the gradual liberal-ization of the prison regime since the 1920s. Solitary confinement under a rule of silence produced few security problems — less than one prisoner in 1,000 managed to escape in 1895. It is interesting to compare that figure with the number of escapes and attempted escapes during a six-year period in the 1930s and in the 1960s (Table IV).

Table IV

Escapes and attempts to escape per 1,000 of the daily average population of prisons, borstals and detention centres:

1930	8.4	1960	56.8
1931	8.0	1961	58.7
1932	7.1	1962	49.1
1933	14.3	1963	54.6
1934	11.9	1964	72.0
1935	9.1	*1965	63.2
1936	13.1	1966	58.4

*From 1965, figures were broken down into three categories: escapes, attempts, and escapes while at other establishments.
(*Source: The English Prison Officer since 1850*, J. E. Thomas, 1972)

The years 1965 - 6 produced a number of sensational escapes. In 1965, a gang of men managed to remove Ronald Biggs, one of the Great Train Robbers, from Wandsworth Prison. Then, in 1966, George Blake escaped from Wormwood Scrubs. Blake had been imprisoned for espionage, and his escape was viewed as a serious breach of national security. As a result, Lord Mountbatten was appointed to undertake a full-scale inquiry into prison security.

His main criticism concerned the apparent lack of communication between the Home Office Prison Department (which had replaced the old Prison Commission in 1963) and prison governors and staff. Measures suggested to improve security included closed circuit television and the provision of a special security guard to patrol the prison perimeter, with the aid of trained dogs.

Mountbatten's suggestions for dealing with 'high security risks', which became more crucial after the abolition of capital punishment in 1965, were taken into consideration in the framing of the Criminal Justice Act of 1967.

The Criminal Justice Act, 1967

Classification of prisoners The Home Office accepted the Mountbatten Report's recommendations that prisoners should be classified according to the extent to which they present a security risk. Four categories, A, B, C, D, were established. Category A designates prisoners who should not on any account

53 Lord Mountbatten, appointed to lead an inquiry into prison security, visits Wormwood Scrubs a few days after George Blake's sensational escape in 1966.

54 Training in building skills equips offenders with a useful trade and also reduces the cost to the tax-payer of the construction of new prisons (1971).

be allowed to escape. Category B denotes medium security risks. Prisoners classed in categories C and D present little or no security risk and might be considered suitable for open institutions.

Maximum security units The Home Office rejected Lord Mountbatten's suggestion that a special maximum security prison should be built for high-risk offenders. Instead, it decided that such prisoners should be dispersed in maximum security units set aside in existing prisons.

Corrective Training and *Preventive Detention* were abolished. Little use had been made by the courts of the former, and the latter had not solved the problem of persistent offenders. However, it was still the case that persistent offenders would continue to receive long sentences, and their rehabilitation remains a serious problem.

Suspended sentences The courts were empowered to suspend a sentence of up to two years' imprisonment, for between one and three years. If the offender committed a further offence during this period, the suspension order was revoked, and the sentence would have to be served. However, the courts were obliged to suspend the sentence if the period of imprisonment was six months or less.

Probation and after-care The act unified the administration of the probation and after-care of offenders, placing it under the control of one authority, the Probation and After-care Service.

Juvenile offenders The treatment of juvenile offenders remained largely unchanged except that the act recognized the need to include more education and social training in the detention centres' regime. The main policy changes towards juvenile offenders came two years later, with the Children and Young Persons Act of 1969.

This act, designed to be implemented by stages, carried the non-punitive approach to the treatment of juvenile offenders further than previous legislation. It looks forward to the day when no child under the age of 14 will be prosecuted except for homicide. Basically, juvenile delinquents are no longer seen as young criminals in need of punishment, but rather as young members of a much larger group who, for a variety of reasons, are in need of 'care and control'. The Children and Young Persons Act has been attacked in some quarters and there are pressures for it to be amended. The value of its humane approach should not, however, be underestimated.

Prison Conditions Today

The Home Office publication, *People in Prison* (1968), is a useful guide to what the Prison Department is trying to do to improve the prison regime, and touches on some of the problems encountered in the process. In theory an offender is considered to have paid a sufficient price for what he has done by being deprived of his liberty. The aim, therefore, is to make conditions in prison as humane as possible within the constraints imposed by the need for security.

Employment According to *People in Prison*, their main aim is 'that offenders in custody shall be given training and experience that will fit them to get and keep jobs on discharge'. Secondly, 'that the best possible economic use should be made of prison labour'.

Devising employment suitable for individuals with widely varying interests, skills and aptitudes, as well as lengths of sentence, is not easy. Other factors which hamper the quality and scope of employment are overcrowding, old, unsuitable buildings, shortage of staff and the need for security.

To date the policy has been to concentrate on semi-skilled industry, including light engineering, carpentry, tailoring etc. For those in open institutions, there is scope for outdoor occupations, such as farming and building work. If the necessary supervision can be provided, parties of prisoners may be employed by local farmers or in work for the community.

Education Education in prisons was not placed on a proper, professionally organized basis until 1948, when the Prison Commission arranged for the local authorities to take over responsibility for prison education, and appointed a director of education and welfare to co-ordinate policy. Today most prisons have an education officer who is responsible for organizing courses with the aid of full- and part-time teachers. Attendance at classes is not compulsory except for prisoners under 21.

The range of courses includes a variety of academic and technical subjects, and prisoners may study for national examinations at school or university level. Many prisoners, however, can neither read nor write, and for them special classes are provided. An illiterate prisoner is obviously doubly disadvantaged when he tries to find employment on discharge, and so this aspect of education in prisons has a particular importance.

While it would be wrong to underestimate the value of better educational qualifications, perhaps the most important thing about prison education is that it is, at least for adults, entirely optional. Prisoners have extremely little opportunity to express their individual likes and dislikes, and so freedom to decide whether to study and what to study takes on a special significance.

Religion In the past, the prison chaplain had to be something of a 'jack of all trades' — he ran the education of the prison and was responsible for the moral and social training of offenders. Today, other people have been brought in to do much of this work, and the prison chaplain is now more like a parish priest, with the prison as his parish. Special provision is made for prisoners of various religious denominations.

Diet and clothing Since the war, much has been done to improve the prison catering service, and in some prisons communal dining areas have been provided. However, it is still quite common for prisoners to have to collect their meals and carry them back to their cells to eat.

Prison clothing has become less institutionalized. The old 'battledress blouse' formerly issued to men has been replaced by a jacket, and women are generally allowed considerable freedom to choose their own clothes.

Medical care Each prison has its own 'sick bay', but there are special prison hospitals for those who need them. There is a separate prison medical service and National Health Service facilities may also be used.

The most important change in prison medical care since the war has been the increased use of psychiatric treatment. Offenders who suffer from severe mental disorders, and who must, for their own sake and that of the general public, be kept in secure conditions, are confined in one of the special psychiatric hospitals — Broadmoor, Moss Side and Rampton. These hospitals are not restricted to prisoners and are controlled by the Ministry of Health.

The number of offenders who are severely mentally disturbed is, however, small. On the other hand, a sizeable number of prisoners are found to be in need of some kind of psychiatric treatment. This is hardly surprising, in view of the increasing number of people outside prison who are currently receiving treatment of this kind.

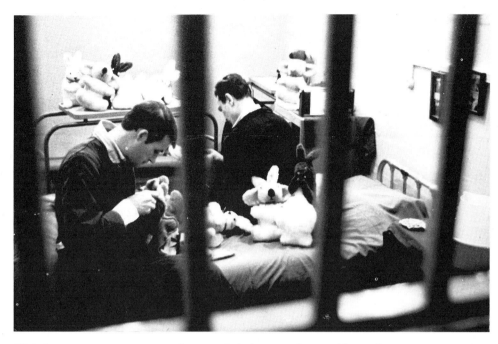

55 Prisoners at Dartmoor spend some of their spare time making soft toys.

56 Lord Stonham, at one time Under-Secretary of State at the Home Office, joins prisoners at breakfast during a visit to the maximum security prison at Blundeston, Suffolk.

In 1962, the first psychiatric prison at Grendon in Buckinghamshire was opened. Grendon holds only 150 prisoners out of an average prison population of over 30,000. It is unique in that for each prisoner there is virtually one member of staff. Grendon is a maximum security establishment, but tight security has enabled the most humane and permissive regime to be introduced. The prisoners are of all types and ages. All are being given the opportunity, principally by discussing their problems, to come to terms with themselves. However, doubts are beginning to be expressed about its success.

Prisoner - Staff Relationships

The mere fact of being imprisoned together creates a bond among prisoners and leads to the formation of a separate and distinct community — a world within a world. This is not mainly because the prisoners are all law-breakers of one kind or another. It is an instinctive reaction among people who are held captive against their will, as prisoners of war over the centuries have demonstrated. Constantly under surveillance by the custodial staff, the prisoner community nevertheless manages to lead a private, separate existence, with its own code of behaviour, its own disciplinary rules and its own ties of loyalty.

The tensions produced by a 'them and us' relationship of the kind found in prison are increased if there is also a lack of harmony within the prison staff itself. During the twentieth century, and especially since the last war, changes in the prison regime and in the treatment of prisoners upset the normal equilibrium, however precarious, which existed between prisoners and members of the prison staff. In order to carry out the new policy of rehabilitation, increasing numbers of non-uniformed staff were brought into the prisons. For a long time, the uniformed prison officers had harboured grievances. They were understaffed and overworked; their pay was small and their prospects of promotion few. Their resentment grew when it seemed that they were also being excluded from the more interesting and socially rewarding work being done in the prisons. This made them feel out of sympathy with the new approach to the treatment of prisoners.

It soon became clear that the prison officers needed to share as far as possible in the social work being done in the prisons. The importance of including courses in basic psychology in the officers' training programme has now been recognized. To turn this theory into practice, group therapy or group counselling has been introduced in many prisons.

People argue that prison officers are not adequately trained for this work and that one should not try to combine the conflicting roles of custodial officer and therapist. However, the use of group counselling does seem on balance to have improved the relationship and reduced tension between staff and prisoners.

Prisoners' Contacts with the Outside World

Prisoners are allowed to write a specified number of letters weekly and to receive a limited number of supervised visits. The allocation of letters and

57 A group counselling session in progress at Holloway Prison (1964).

58 This picture shows a number of prisoners' wives and supporters demonstrating outside Wandsworth for an inquiry into conditions in the prison (1972).

visits is generally better in the training and open prisons than in the local prisons. If a family crisis occurs, the prison governor may allow a prisoner extra letters and visits.

Prisoners serving relatively long sentences may be allowed one or two periods of home leave towards the end of the sentence. Inevitably, marriages are likely to suffer when husband or wife is detained in prison for a long time. In some countries, 'conjugal visits' are allowed and special facilities provided so that visiting spouses may stay overnight. However, for various reasons — not least the problem of providing temporary married quarters — the Home Office prefers home leave to conjugal visits.

Unfortunately, many prisoners have no family, or have been rejected by their relatives, or are single people without friends. For such prisoners, visits from members of the prison visitors' associations which exist all over the country are very important. Useful friendships may be formed which stand the offender in good stead when he is discharged.

Probation and After-Care

Anyone who is subjected to the disciplined regime of an institution for any length of time becomes cushioned against the responsibilities of daily life. Over the months or years, the prisoner has lost the habit of taking decisions. The return to freedom for a prisoner is almost always a bewildering experience and frequently a terrifying one. He is bombarded by sights, sounds and smells for which the seclusion and uniformity of prison life have left him unprepared. He may be overwhelmed by problems — where to live, how to find a job, how to fill in forms, make a phone call and so on. For many ex-prisoners, the whole business is too much and so they sidestep the problem by committing another offence which will ensure that they return to the security of prison.

Any efforts which have been made in prison to rehabilitate an offender may be completely wasted if he is not given support to tide him over the difficult period immediately after discharge. Such help is provided today by the Probation and After-care Service. It should be stressed that after-care is entirely optional for the vast majority of offenders. Only certain kinds of prisoner — those under 21 at the time of sentencing and those released early on licence or parole — are legally obliged to be placed under the supervision of a probation officer. There is evidence, however, that more and more prisoners are taking advantage of the after-care service on a purely voluntary basis.

Although the emphasis is on the period after discharge, the aim of probation and after-care is ideally to provide a certain continuity of treatment, a kind of 'through-care'. The probation officer first meets the prisoner in court, becomes acquainted with his problems and helps to deal with any family or other matters which may be worrying him. During imprisonment, contact with the prisoner is maintained, and the probation officer can act as a kind of go-between, between the offender and his family — at this stage it is usually the family, rather than the prisoner, who needs the greater support. By the time the prisoner is discharged, a useful relationship should have been built up between him and the probation officer. In reality, probation officers are usually over-worked and cannot always give to an individual prisoner the amount of un-divided attention he needs. It is also difficult to maintain continuity; staff changes may prevent the same probation officer from seeing a particular case through to the end.

Volunteers, or 'associates' as they are called, can help by dealing with some of the day-to-day difficulties offenders encounter on release, thus freeing the probation officer for work on the more intractable problems.

Voluntary Organizations

Before the government took over the responsibility for providing after-care, the work was done by voluntary Discharged Prisoners' Aid Societies. In 1966, the National Association for the Care and Resettlement of Offenders (NACRO) was created out of the old National Association of Discharged Prisoners' Aid Societies.

NACRO helps ex-offenders in all kinds of ways. It runs its own hostel scheme to ease the problem of finding accommodation, and has improved opportunities for employment. It encourages self-help among discharged prisoners, and has also been able to provide specialist treatment facilities for those with particular problems such as alcoholism, gambling or drug abuse. Since its formation, NACRO has also become an important pressure group in seeking changes in penal policy.

The Apex Trust was formed in 1967 and is wholly concerned with im-proving employment prospects for discharged offenders. Apex wanted to see whether finding suitable jobs for offenders would reduce the number of reconvictions. Their first experimental study, carried out at Wormwood Scrubs and Pentonville with 450 men, was disappointing. It seemed by 1970 that Apex had made little or no impact on the reconviction rate. Since then, Apex has concentrated its efforts on finding work for a limited range of offenders, those convicted of 'white-collar' crimes — fraud, or embezzlement — and sex offences. By 1972, the number of successful placings had risen to 30 per cent compared with 19 per cent two years earlier. This is at least a hopeful start for a new approach to the problem of finding work for ex-prisoners.

Current Trends

The twentieth century has witnessed a steady growth in the number of offences which the police know have been committed; the increase has been particularly marked since the Second World War. The number of offences involving violence to the person has risen and in recent years there have also been bomb attacks in London and other parts of the country. This disturbing increase in the level of violence has caused some people to react against 'soft' measures and to advocate a more punitive approach to the sentencing and treatment of offenders. There have been demands for a return to corporal punishment and for the re-introduction of the death penalty, at least for those responsible for the murder of police officers or for indiscriminate killings arising from acts of terrorism.

On the other hand, reform groups, such as the Howard League and NACRO, feel that the temptation to return to more severe penalties should be resisted. They point out that, in the past, neither a harsh criminal code nor a repressive prison regime has ever succeeded in deterring people from committing crimes or from being reconvicted. Admittedly, the crime rate and the number of people in custody have never been greater. However, this is used to support the argument that imprisonment itself does not deter, and, indeed, frequently ensures that an offender will stick to a life of crime. It is felt that a new radical approach is needed.

This view is strongly supported by the organization Radical Alternatives to Prison (RAP) and by the newly formed Preservation of the Rights of Prisoners group (PROP). Prisoners feel that they are particularly qualified by their own personal experience to criticize and to suggest improvements in penal policy, and it is true that until recently virtually no attention has been paid to their views.

In fact, the Prison Department would be only too glad to see a reduction in the prison population, if only to ease the chronic problem of overcrowding. In 1972, fresh alternatives to imprisonment were introduced by the Criminal Justice Act, which provided for the establishment of Community Service Centres and Day-Training Centres. The object of these centres, which are still in an experimental stage, is to treat offenders in the community by providing employment, support and supervision. This kind of treatment seems likely to develop further as time goes on, but there will always be a number of offenders for whom prisons will still be needed.

59 Prison corridors, Wandsworth. Improving conditions is difficult while prisoners still have to be accommodated in Victorian buildings.

Conclusion

In studying the history of British prisons, one is struck by the frequent far-sightedness of legislators and by the dedication and humanity of the many unselfish men and women who have tried to improve the lot of prisoners over the centuries. But one is also moved by the sheer waste of human lives, and by the appalling degradation and suffering inflicted over the years on the vast majority of prisoners, most of whom were neither murderers nor violent criminals, but just rather inadequate people unable to cope with everyday life.

In 1794, the then Lord Chancellor of England wrote: 'It is not so much for want of *good laws*, as from their *inexecution*, that the state of the prisons is so bad.' His verdict still holds true to some extent today. It is easy enough to legislate, but unless the will and the resources to implement them are there, the best laws will remain just good intentions. Progress is still hampered by out-of-date buildings, overcrowding, the chronic shortage of staff and money and, not least, by the indifference of the general public towards those who have been 'inside'. Until the community as a whole cares enough about what happens to the 35,000 and more human lives which go to waste in prison each year, the rehabilitation of society's 'socially sick' members is likely to remain a discouragingly slow process.

Suggestions for Further Reading

Newspapers and periodicals are a constant source of information on prisons past and present. Local societies occasionally produce pamphlets of interest — for example, C. E. Cooper has written a booklet about prisoners of war during the Napoleonic War, *Prisoners at Porchester* (Portsmouth Museums Society, 1973, obtainable from the Business Manager, 28 East Cosham Road, Portsmouth). Libraries will usually have records of Quarter and Petty Sessions which are full of information about prisoners and punishments. The local Record Office may also have useful documentary material. Essex County Council has, for instance, produced a Teaching Portfolio, *Law and Order in Essex, 1066-1874*, obtainable from Essex Record Office, County Hall, Chelmsford.

Brian Ashley, *Law and Order*, Past-into-Present Series, Batsford, 1971.

Ray Jenkins, *The Lawbreakers*, Connexions, Penguin Education, 1971.

Ralph B. Pugh, *Imprisonment in Medieval England*, Cambridge University Press, 1968.

John Bellamy, *Crime and Public Order in England in the Later Middle Ages*, Routledge & Kegan Paul, 1973.

S. and B. Webb, *English Prisons under Local Government*, Longman, 1922; Frank Cass, 1963. From Howard to Ruggles-Brise. A classic work.

Ann D. Smith, *Women in Prison: A Study in Penal Methods*, Steven & Sons, 1962. Middle Ages to the present day; good on Holloway and Askham Grange Open Prison.

R. S. E. Hinde, *The British Penal System, 1773-1950*, Duckworth, 1951. Useful on juvenile offenders and the Criminal Justice Act, 1948.

D. L. Howard, *The English Prisons: Their Past and Their Future*, Methuen, 1960. Very readable survey — nineteenth and twentieth centuries.

People in Prison in England and Wales, HMSO, 1969. Present policy outlined; Criminal Justice Act, 1967; statistics, prisons list, etc.

A. G. L. Shaw, *Convicts and the Colonies: A Study of Penal Transportation from Great Britain and Ireland to Australia and other parts of the British Empire*, Faber, 1966.

Joyce Marlow, *The Tolpuddle Martyrs*, Andre Deutsch, 1971; Panther 1974. Well-told story of George Loveless and five other trade unionists who were transported to Australia in 1834.

W. Branch Johnson, *The Prison Hulks*, Christopher Johnson, 1957; revised edition, Phillimore, 1970. Prisoner of war hulks included.

A. L. Rowse, *The Tower of London in the History of the Nation*, Weidenfeld and Nicolson, 1972; Sphere Books, Cardinal, 1974.

Anthony Babington, *The English Bastille: A History of Newgate and Prison Conditions in Britain, 1188-1902*, Macdonald, 1971. A fascinating book; numerous contemporary quotations.

D. L. Howard, *John Howard: Prison Reformer*, Christopher Johnson, 1958.

Janet Whitney, *Elizabeth Fry*, Harrap, 1937.

John Kent, *Elizabeth Fry*, Batsford, 1962.

Elizabeth Fry and Prison Reform, Jackdaw No. 63, Jonathan Cape.

Charles Dickens, *Sketches by Boz*, 1837. (See *Scenes*, Chapter 24, Criminal Courts and Chapter 25, A Visit to Newgate.)

Charles Dickens, *American Notes*, 1842. (See Chapter 7, Philadelphia and its Solitary Prison.)

Charles Dickens, *Little Dorrit*, 1857. Novel set in the Marshalsea.

H. Mayhew and J. Binny, *The Criminal Prisons of London and Scenes of Prison Life*, 1862; reprinted by Frank Cass, 1968. Invaluable.

J. J. Tobias, *Nineteenth Century Crime: Prevention and Punishment*, David & Charles, 1972. A collection of edited documents.

J. E. Thomas, *The English Prison Officer since 1850: A Study in Conflict*, Routledge & Kegan Paul, 1972.

S. K. Ruck, *Paterson on Prisons*, Muller, 1951.

Roger Hood, *Borstal Re-assessed*, Heinemann, 1965.

Martin Davies, *Prisoners of Society: Attitudes and After-care*, Routledge & Kegan Paul, 1974. Probation and after-care service.

Tony Parker, *A Man of Good Abilities*, Hutchinson, 1967. The diary of an ex-prisoner; his conversations with the author.

M. Berlins and G. Wansell, *Caught in the Act: Children, Society and the Law*, Penguin, 1974.

Index

The numbers in **bold** refer to the figure numbers of the illustrations.